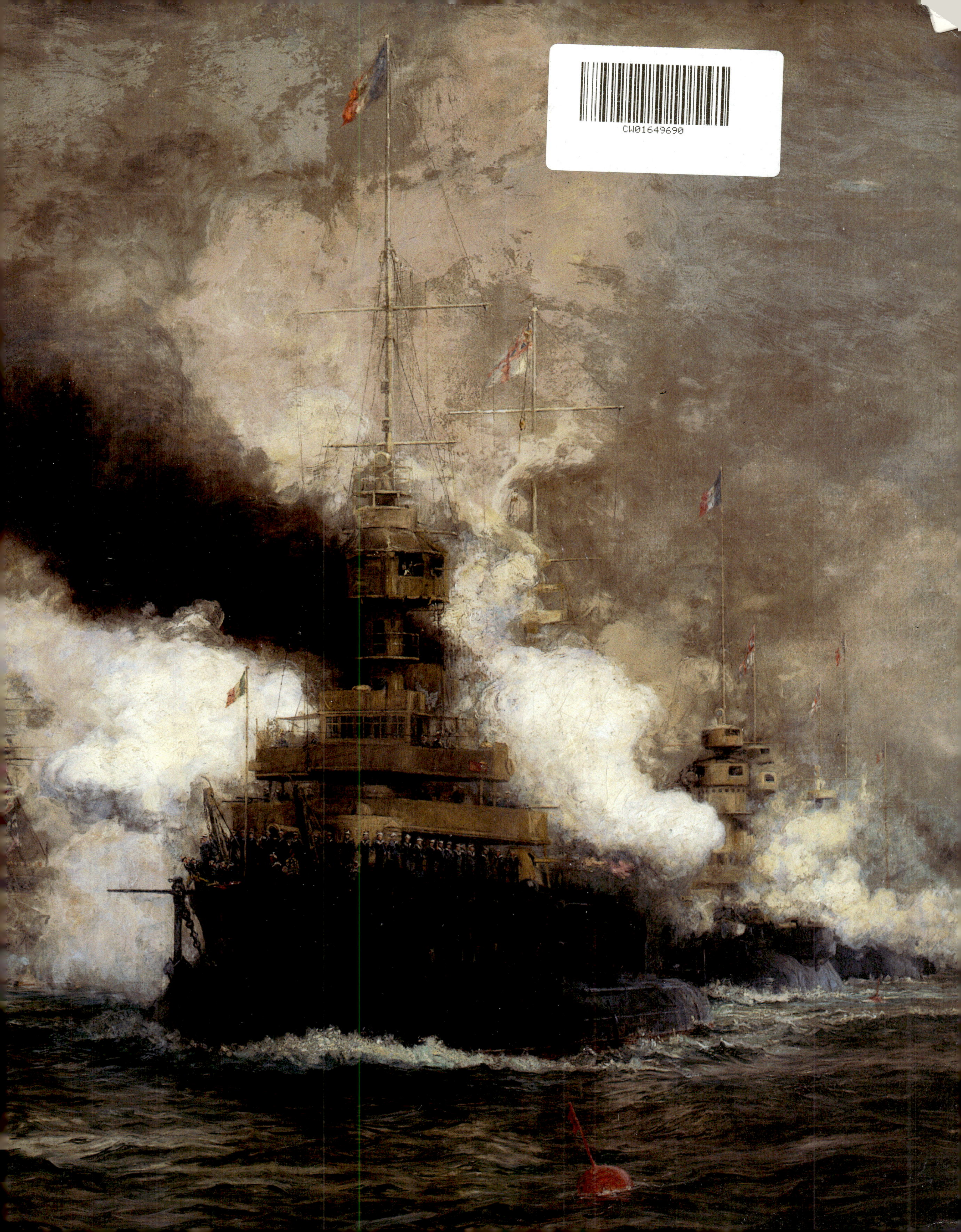

8 & 10 Ryder Street
St James's
London SW1Y 6QB
Telephone: 020 7839 7551
Facsimile: 020 7839 1603
gallery@chrisbeetles.com
www.chrisbeetles.com

ISBN 1 871136 85 7

Text by David Wootton and signed contributors
Edited by Edwina Freeman
Indices by David Wootton
Design by Jeremy Brook at Graphic Ideas
Photography by Red Apple
Digital Photography by Philip Tite
Colour separation and printing by Waterside Press Ltd

Cataloguing in Publication Data is available from the British Library

Cover: Edward Seago – see page 39
Front Endpapers: William Lionel Wyllie – see page 22
Back Endpapers: Alfred William Hunt – see page 14
Title Page: Janet Cumbrae Stewart – see page 32

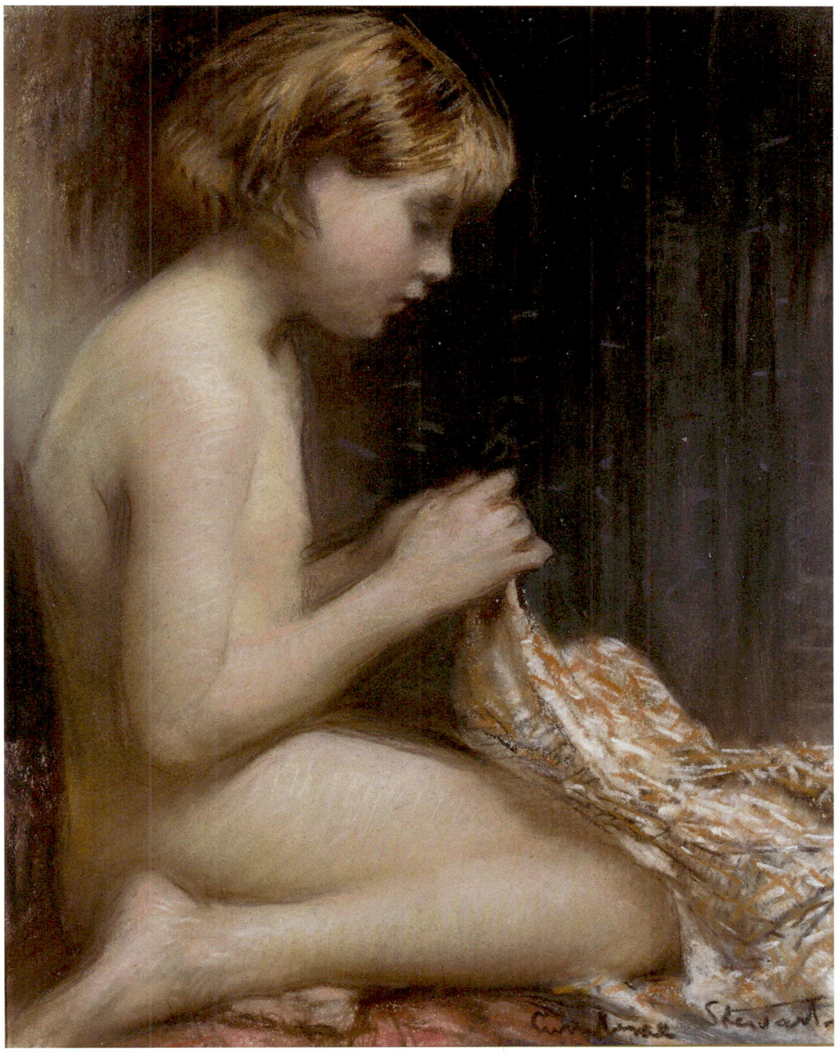

Chris Beetles

Summer Show

2004

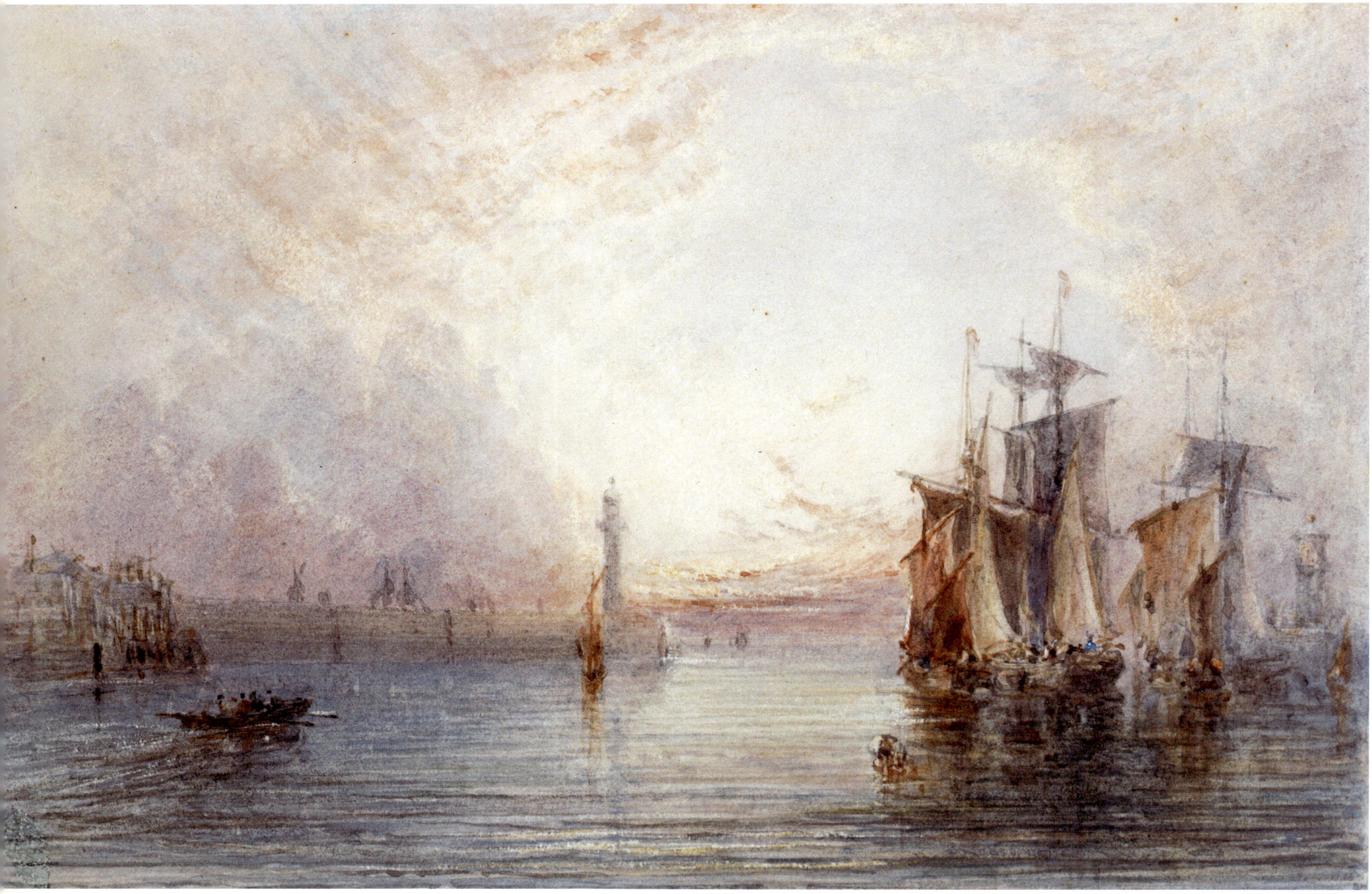

1. Vessel Leaving Harbour – Evening *inscribed with title, watercolour, 3 ¾ x 5 ½ inches*

George Weatherill

George Weatherill (1810–1890)

Turner of the North

George Weatherill was born in Staithes, Yorkshire, on 18 September 1810. During his apprenticeship to a solicitor, he became acquainted with George Haydock Dodgson, a local painter, who discovered and developed his artistic talent. At the age of twenty, he moved to Whitby to work for another solicitor, later joining the staff of the bankers, Simpson and Chapman. Yet he painted whenever possible, even rising early to study the sunrise. Once his position in the bank was assured, he was occasionally sent to London on business, and was eventually promoted to Chief Cashier. During his stays in the capital, he would visit the National Gallery, and became so inspired by the example of J M W Turner as to make a number of engravings of his work. As if to emphasise both his quality and his status as a resolutely local artist, he was dubbed the 'Turner of the North'. He exhibited a mere half dozen pictures in metropolitan exhibitions, and was mainly patronised by Northern industrialists and merchants. The pressure of balancing two careers led him to have a nervous breakdown and, in 1860, at the age of fifty, he resigned from the bank. On regaining his health, he returned to painting and soon earned more from painting alone than he had from banking and painting together. He died on 30 August 1890 and was buried in Whitby cemetery. In turn, his application to his work encouraged his children to become artists.

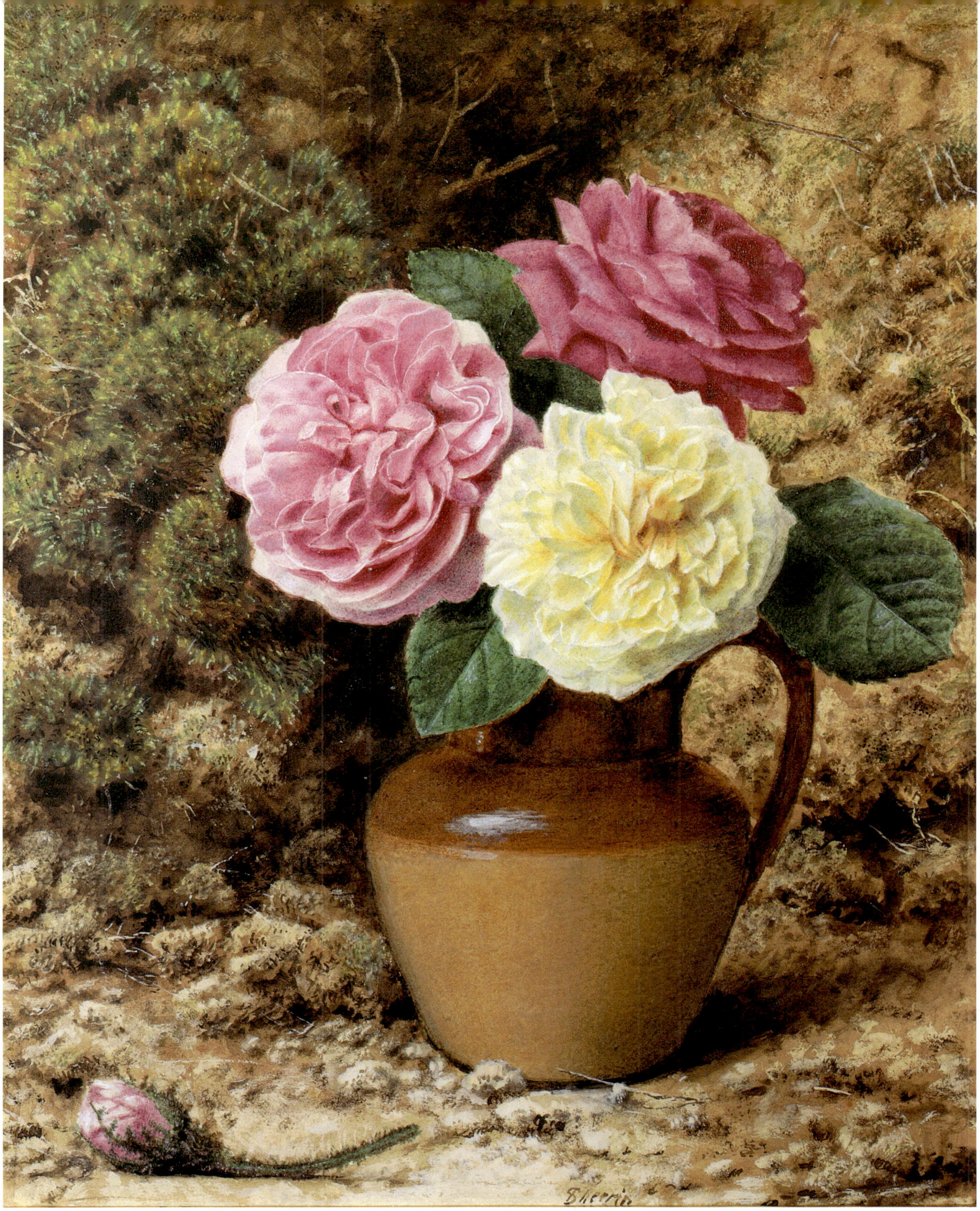

2. Roses in a Jug *signed, watercolour with bodycolour, 12 x 9 ½ inches*

John Sherrin

John Sherrin RI (1819–1896)

John Sherrin was born in London. One of the few known pupils of William Henry Hunt, he equalled his master as a painter of intimate still life compositions, and also depicted animals. He was apprenticed to Samuel Smith, a jeweller, and later worked for the designers Howell & James and the diamond merchants Matthews & Peake. He was left a considerable fortune by Matthews. From 1859 until his death, he exhibited at the Royal Academy, the Royal Society of British Artists and the Royal Institute of Painters in Water-Colours. He was elected an associate of the Royal Institute in 1866 and a full member thirteen years later. He died in Ramsgate.

William Simpson

William Simpson RI (1823–1899)

William Simpson was born in Glasgow on 28 October 1823, and educated in that city and in Perth. Intending to become an engineer, he spent some time in an architect's office, but was then apprenticed to a local firm of lithographers. Moving to London in 1851, he was employed by the printers Day & Son. He worked as a Special Artist, producing graphic reports from the front-line on a number of exciting assignments. He claimed to be the first Special Artist to be involved in action. He was sent to the Baltic by Colnaghi to record the naval battles which instigated the Crimean War, and arrived in the Crimea itself in 1854, only two weeks after the Battle of Inkerman. The resulting lithographic folio, *Illustrations of the War in the East*, was the first of his many books; its success led to his being known as 'Crimean Simpson'. In the same period, he toured Circassia with the Duke of Newcastle. He spent three years in India between 1859 and 1862, in the aftermath of the Mutiny, making architectural and archaeological sketches, and visiting Kashmir and Tibet.

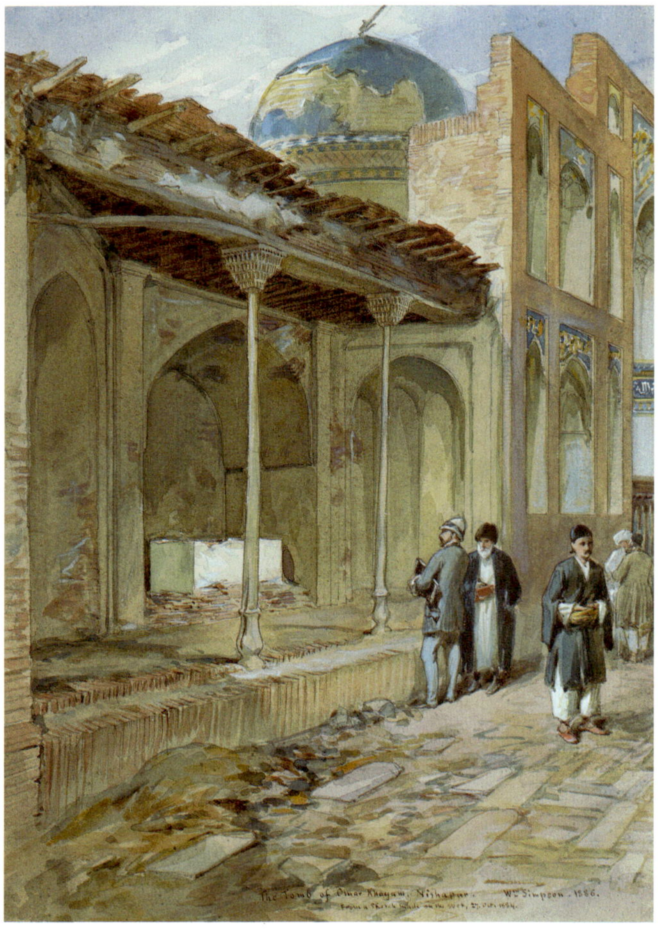

3. The Tomb of Omar Khayam, Nishapur

signed, inscribed with title and 'From a sketch made on the spot, 27 Oct. 1884' and dated 1886, watercolour with pencil and bodycolour, 11 ¼ x 9 ½ inches

A similar watercolour from the same viewpoint was illustrated in George Eyre-Todd (Editor), *The Autobiography of William Simpson, RI (Crimean Simpson)*, London: T Fisher Unwin, 1903, facing page 306

In 1866, Day & Son went bankrupt, and Simpson began to work for the *Illustrated London News*. He was sent to St Petersburg to record the marriage of the future Czar Alexander III, and also toured Russia with the Prince of Wales, taking in Jerusalem on his return journey. Through the late 1860s and the 1870s he increased the rate of his travels. In 1868 he accompanied Napier on his expedition to Abyssinia, and in 1869 was present at the opening of the Suez Canal. He covered the Franco-Prussian War in 1870, and the resulting Paris Commune. In 1872 he went to China for the wedding of the Emperor, returning via Japan and America. He was in India with the Prince of Wales in 1875, Asia Minor in 1877 and Afghanistan in 1878-79 and 1884-85.

Though Simpson worked chiefly in monochrome for his assignments, he exhibited a number of watercolours and oils, from 1874, at the Royal Society of British Artists and the New Society of Painters in Water-Colours. Elected an associate of the NWS in 1874 and a full member five years later, he was instrumental in transforming the society into the Royal Institute of Painters in Water-Colours in 1883. He then settled in Willesden and devoted himself to writing. He died in London on 17 April 1899. His autobiography was published posthumously in 1903.

The Tomb of Omar Khayam

In 1884, after Russia's encroachment into Central Asia, the Afghan Boundary Commission was set up to define and map the borders between Afghan and Russian territory. The commission was led by General Sir Peter Lumsden, a friend of Simpson; this explains how Simpson managed to attach himself to the party despite the rule that no members of the press would be allowed.

Simpson recounts in his autobiography:

> *At Nishapur Sir Peter arranged that the mehmander should take us to the tomb of Omar Khayam* [1048-1131], *the astronomer poet of Persia... the central part of the monument, that under the blue dome, contains the body of the Imam Reza, the eighth Imam* [died 817]. *It was built in the time of the Shah Sultan Hassan Suffawer. There are two wings in the front, and we were led to the left, where, in a recess formed by the wing, is a plain oblong mass of brick, plastered, with no ornament. This was the tomb of Omar Khayam.* (George Eyre-Todd (editor), *The Autobiography of William Simpson, RI (Crimean Simpson)*, London: T Fisher Unwin, 1903, page 305)

Simpson searched for something he could take as a souvenir from the tomb and, not wishing to remove any artefact, he settled on a bunch of rose hips taken from one of the withered rose bushes in the garden. He sent them back to England where they were propagated at Kew Gardens. A cutting from the ensuing rose tree was planted at the funeral of Edward Fitzgerald (1809-1883) the most famous translator of *The Rubaiyat of Omar Khayyam* (1859).

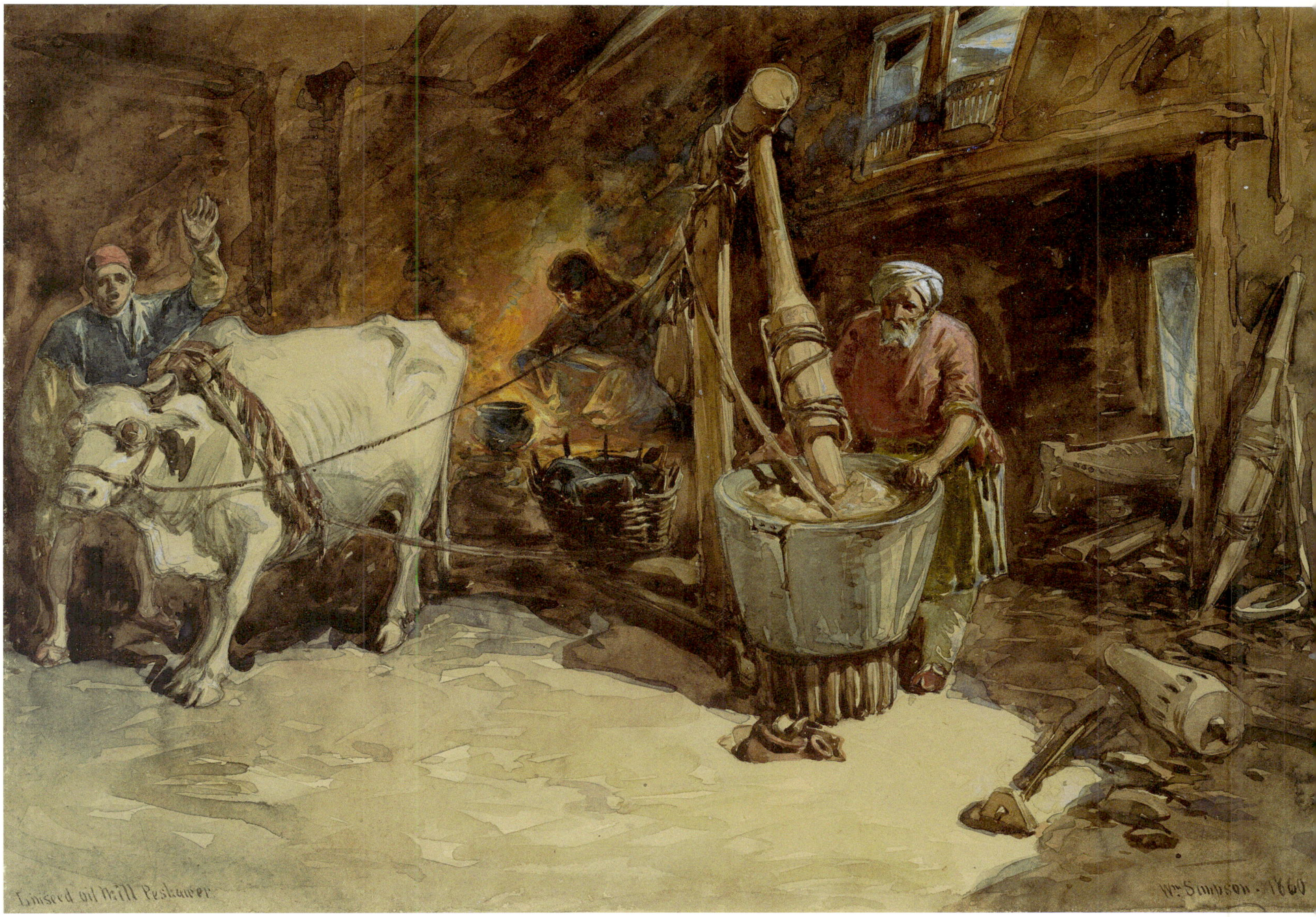

4. Linseed Oil Mill, Peshawer *signed, inscribed with title and dated 1860, watercolour, 10 x 14 inches*

Linseed oil mill, Peshawer

The Indian Mutiny, which ended after more than two years of bloodshed in 1859, had excited the interest of the British public. The printer William Day – encouraged by the sales of Simpson's Crimea book *The Seat of War in the East* (1855/56) which he had printed for Colnaghi's, and the success of David Roberts' book *The Holy Land* (1842-45) with its 250 lithographic illustrations – thought he could revive the flagging fortunes of his business by producing a book on India. Simpson was commissioned to make the illustrations and spent three years travelling in India drawing monuments, landscapes and scenes of everyday Indian life which seemed so exotic to the public at home.

Simpson recounts in his autobiography:

> *At Peshawur I made the acquaintance of Captain Speedy. He had the gift of picking up languages and could speak Pucktoo, the language of the Afghans nearest Peshawur. He went with me to the bazaar, and by his speaking powers got all sorts of fellows to stand and be sketched, Peshawur being a place with a wonderful variety of races and types from India, The Himalayas, Tibet, Afghanistan, and all parts of Central Asia.* (op cit, page 109)

On his return to London, Simpson spent four years finishing 250 watercolours. Many had even been transferred to stone for lithographic reproduction when Day went bankrupt – a complete shock to Simpson who was unaware of Day's financial troubles. He had already paid his own expenses throughout the trip to India and was listed as being owed £2800 by the company, even losing all his watercolours after they were disposed of as bankrupt stock. He wrote, 'This was the big disaster of my life. When the crash came, I was really left a beggar. I had not a penny. Here was the reward of my seven years' work'. (op cit, page 177)

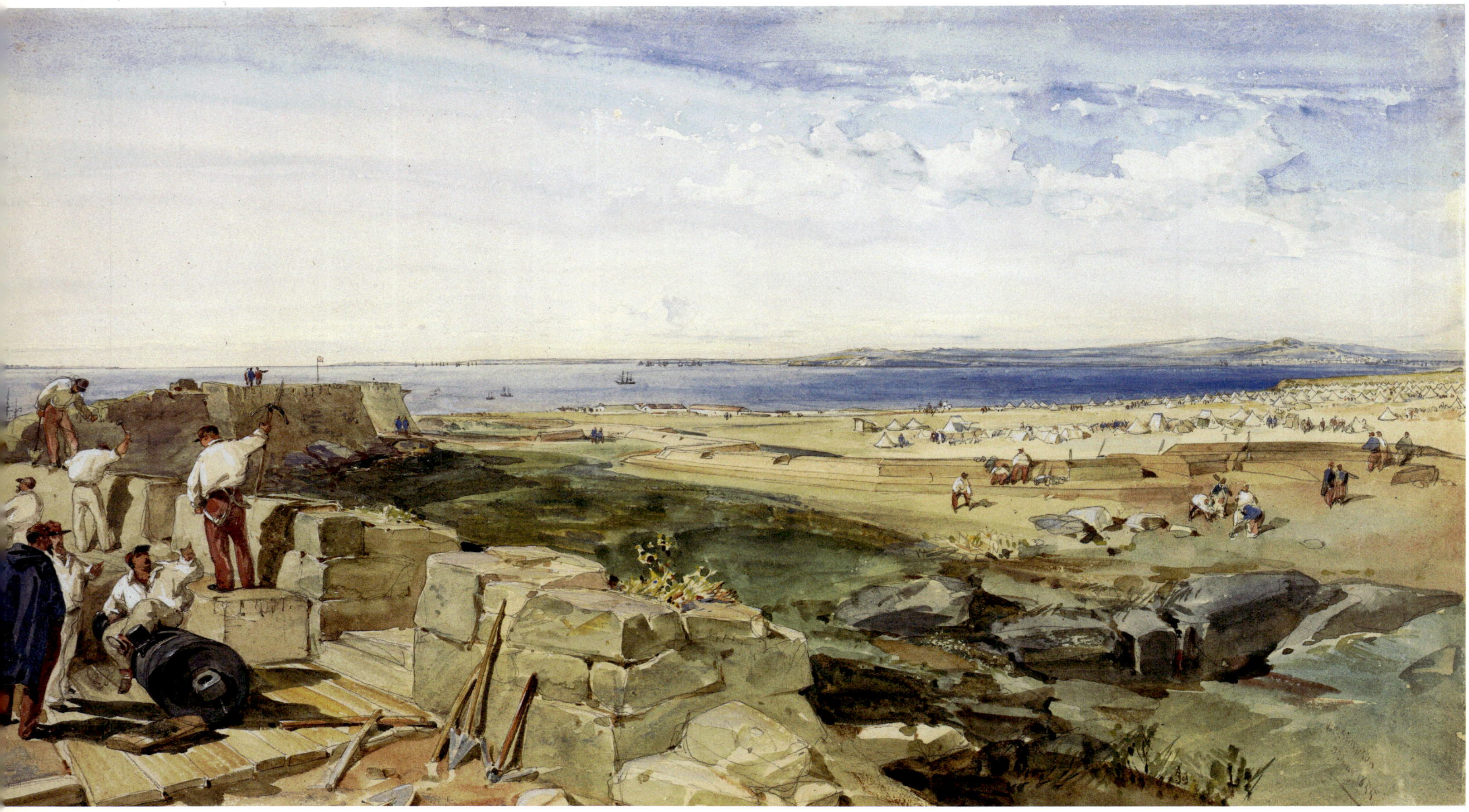

5. Straights of Yenikale with the Bay and Town of Kertch from the old Fortress of Yenikale
signed and dated '3rd June 1855', inscribed 'New Defences, Yenikale' on reverse, watercolour with pencil and bodycolour, 10 ¾ x 19 ¼ inches
Illustrated: William Simpson, *The Seat of War in the East*, London: Paul and Dominic Colnaghi & Co, 1855-56, plate 4

Straits of Yenikale with the Bay and Town of Kertch from the old Fortress of Yenikale

This drawing was made only two weeks after the battle for Kertch and Yenikale during the Crimean War. On 22 May 1855 a combined French, British and Turkish force sailed for Kertch after an abortive attempt earlier in the month. This attack was designed to cut off Russian supplies and open up the Sea of Azov to enable the allied navy to engage enemy coastal supply ships. The attack was very successful; huge quantities of Russian food supplies were destroyed as were guns, ships and an arsenal, with virtually no allied losses. A French garrison was left in Kertch.

The key reproduced [right] from *The Seat of War in the East* shows details of the main features illustrated.
The accompanying text states:

> *This view embraces nearly the whole of the ground crossed by our troops from the point at which they landed, marked by the position of the smaller steamers used for the purpose of transport, over the heights covered with tumuli, through Kertch, round the head of the bay, and into Yenikale, inside whose fortress the spectator is supposed to take his stand.*

Here a party of French soldiers are hard at work, repairing the crumbling walls... Beyond the walls are two new lines of earthworks rapidly approaching completion; the outer one extending from the sea, through the middle of the camp, and surmounted on the top by a very strong redoubt; and the inner line at about half a mile distance from the other. (William Simpson, *The Seat of War in the East*, London: Paul and Dominic Colnaghi & Co, 1855-56, page 88)

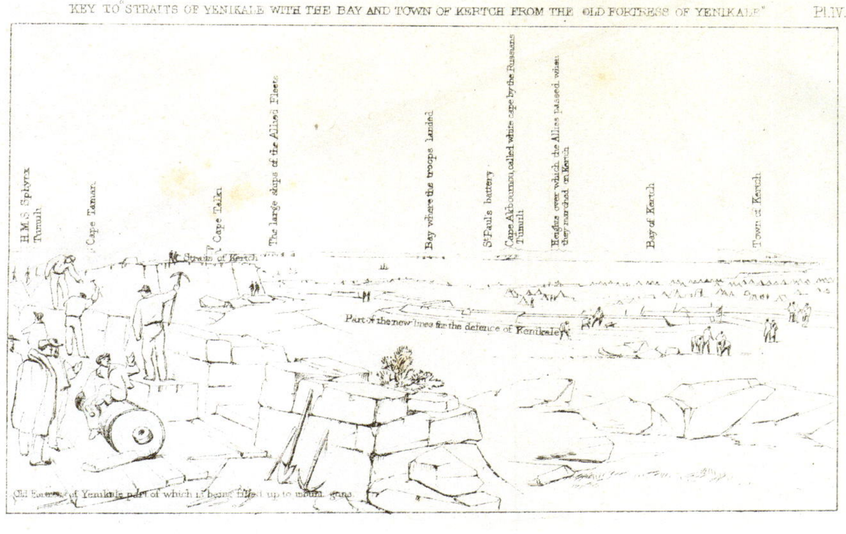

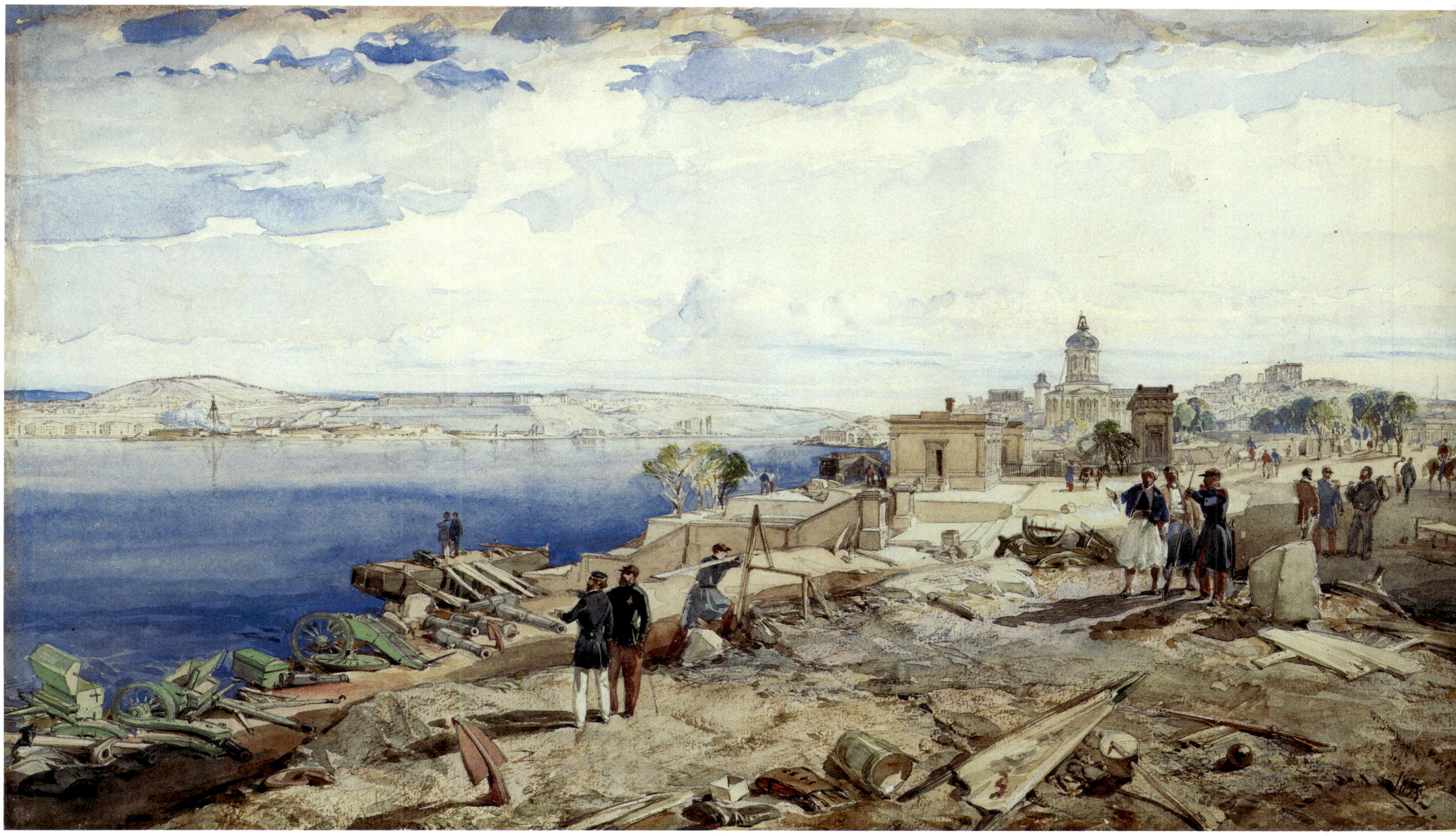

6. Sebastopol from the rear of Fort Nicholas, looking South *signed and dated 'Sept 1855', watercolour, 10 x 14 inches*
Illustrated: William Simpson, *The Seat of War in the East*, London: Paul and Dominic Colnaghi & Co, 1855-56, plate 22

Sebastopol from the rear of Fort Nicholas, looking South

This picture shows most of the key features of the ending of the siege of Sebastopol, after the three-day bombardment of the city starting on 5 September, and the capture of the strategically crucial Malakov by the French and their failure to take Little Redan and the Bastion du Mâs, and the bloody failure of the British at the Redan, all on 8 September 1855, culminating in the Russians evacuating the south of the city a day later.
Although this ended the siege of Sebastopol, deadlock elsewhere eventually led to the end of the Crimean War with Czar Nicholas I accepting Austrian demands in St Petersburg in January 1856 and the ratification of the Treaty of Paris on 27 April of that year.

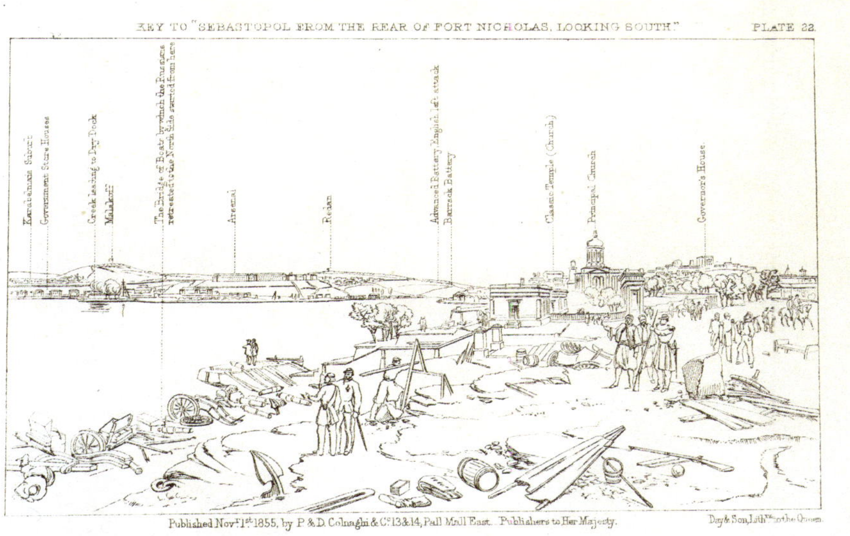

The key reproduced from *The Seat of War in the East* [left] shows the principal features illustrated.
The accompanying text states:

This view supplies a very important deficiency in our estimate of the defences of Sebastopol, by making us acquainted with the rear of the Malakoff and Redan, and their exact position in reference to the Karabelnaya, or that portion of Sebastopol situated on the eastern side of the Inner Harbour, and which contained the Docks, the Arsenal, the Barracks, and the Military Hospital.

All the foreground of this picture... was scattered all over with every variety of article left or dropped in the haste of flight. A number of field artillery guns, which must have been too late to get over, had been tumbled into the sea and were lying in the utmost confusion, with here and there the dirty grey coat of a deceased Ruski, contrasting rather dismally with the bright green of the gun carriages and the blue waves of the Euxine. The stretcher deeply stained with Russian blood lies there, recalling the fearful scenes of the siege. (op cit, pages 107-108)

Notes by Philip Tite

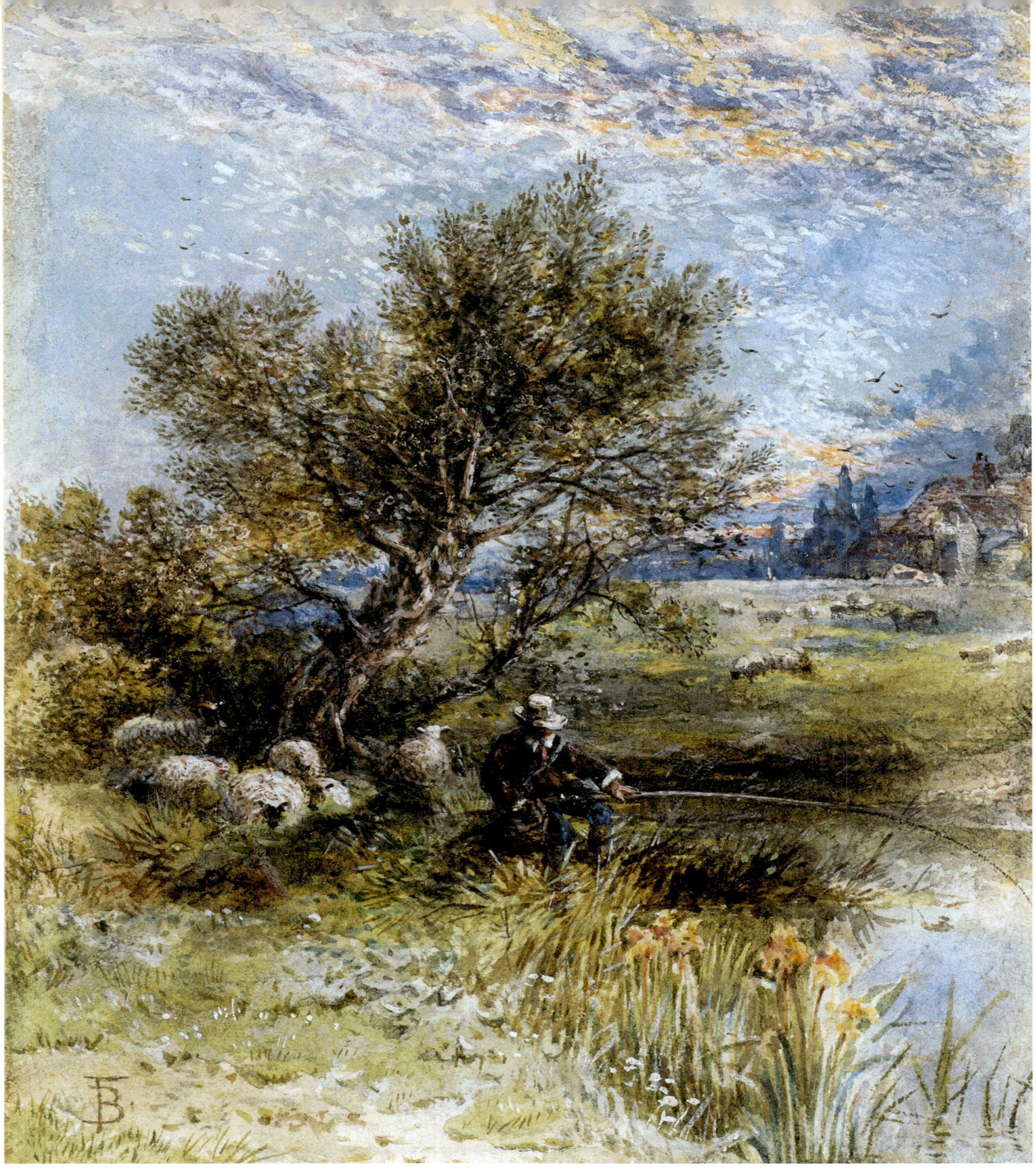

7. The Angler *signed with monogram, watercolour with bodycolour, 5 ½ x 4 ½ inches*
Exhibited: *Birket Foster. Watercolourist & Illustrator:* Towneley Hall Art Gallery & Museums, Burnley, March-May 1999; Warrington Museum & Art Gallery, May-July 1999

Myles Birket Foster

Myles Birket Foster RWS (1825–1899)

Myles Birket Foster was born in Tynemouth, Northumberland on 4 February 1825. He was educated at Quaker schools in Tottenham and Hitchin, and for a short and unsatisfactory period worked in the family brewing business. Fortunately, he was able to convince his parents to allow him to pursue a career in art. He was apprenticed as a wood-engraver, and spent some time under the Northumbrian Ebenezer Landells, the one-time pupil of Thomas Bewick. His first commissions included a beautiful series of initial letters produced for *Punch* (1841-43). From 1846, he worked independently as a black and white illustrator. He began a ten-year relationship with the *Illustrated London News* in 1847, and made his name three years later with vignettes for Longfellow's *Evangeline*. Throughout the 1850s he consolidated his skills, and at the end of the decade worked on colour-printed illustrations with his friend, the printer Edmund Evans. This collaboration developed from Birket Foster's experiments in watercolour. During the same decade he had evolved a flexible stippled technique which enabled him to become one of the few artists to successfully transfer the medium of watercolour to large surfaces, and he looked for means of reproducing his subtleties. He produced landscapes and rustic scenes in the Home Counties and, from the 1850s, painted regularly on the Continent. By 1860, he was exhibiting regularly at the Old Water-Colour Society and was elected an associate member. He became a full member two years later, and from that time worked less regularly as an illustrator. He exhibited oils at the Royal Academy from 1869 and as late as 1895 was elected to the membership of the Berlin Academy. He died on 27 March 1899.

Further reading: Jan Reynolds, *Birket Foster*, London: Batsford, 1984

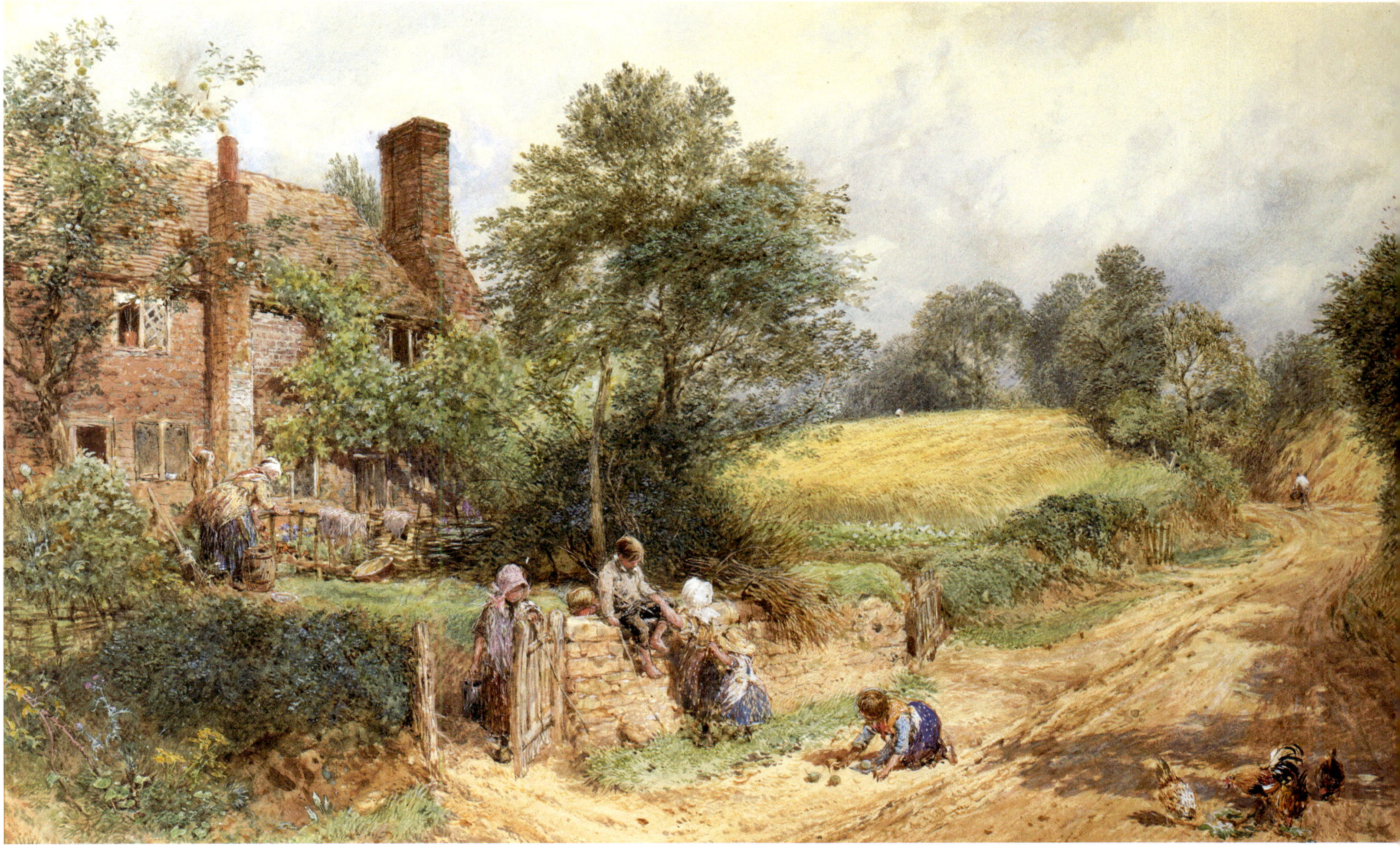

8. A Cottage in Surrey *signed with monogram, watercolour with bodycolour, 8 x 13 inches*

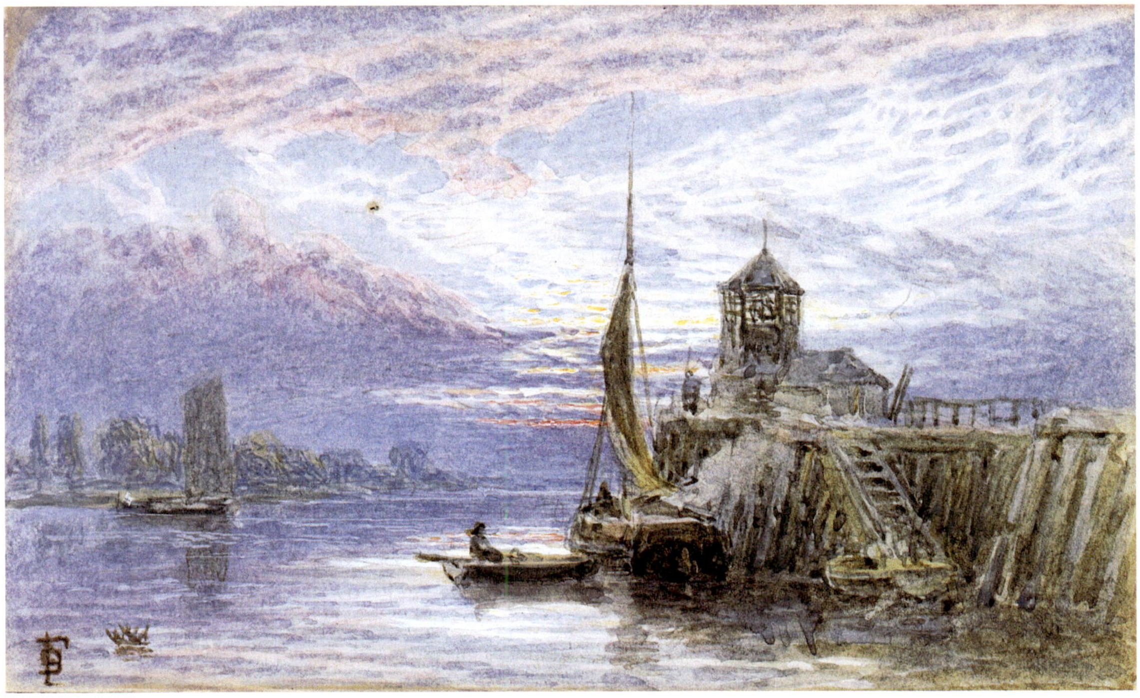

9. A Quay at Dusk
signed with monogram, watercolour with bodycolour and pencil,
2 ¾ x 4 ½ inches

William Holman Hunt

William Holman Hunt OM ARSA RWS (1827–1910)

William Holman Hunt was born on 2 April 1827, the son of a warehouse manager. After a grammar school education he was determined to pursue a career in art and applied for a place at the Royal Academy Schools. He was encouraged to reapply by John Everett Millais whom he had met while sketching at the Academy and was successful on his third attempt in 1844. His 1848 RA exhibit *The Eve of St Agnes* was greatly admired by Dante Gabriel Rossetti, both for its technical skill and its Keatsian subject matter and as a result the two men became friends. They were founder members of the Pre-Raphaelite Brotherhood when it was formed in the September of that year.

Hunt remained true to the principles of the Brotherhood throughout his career, selecting appropriately moralistic subject matter, executed with painstaking accuracy, even travelling in the Holy Land in difficult and sometimes perilous conditions to create realistic landscape backgrounds, figures and detailing for his paintings of religious subjects. Earning him the nickname 'Holy Hunt' some of these pictures were among the most famous and iconic of the period. *The Scapegoat* (1855), *The Shadow of Death* (1873) and *The Triumph of the Innocents* (1887) exemplify this.

In 1860 he completed another such painting, the eagerly-awaited *The Finding of the Saviour in the Temple* which had taken six years to complete. The Belgian dealer Ernest Gambart had an agreement for first refusal on this painting but Hunt had not fixed a price. For this he enrolled the help of Charles Dickens – a notoriously tough business negotiator – who calculated on the basis of time spent on the work a record price for a living artist of 5,500 guineas. Gambart initially refused this unprecedented figure but, realising that Hunt would not negotiate, relented and purchased the painting.

In September of the same year Hunt and Val Prinsep joined Frank Palgrave, Thomas Woolner and Alfred, Lord Tennyson on a walking tour in West Cornwall and the Scilly Isles. Palgrave was working on his anthology, *The Golden Treasury*, and it seems poetry was much discussed. However, the holiday was very productive for the artists, both Prinsep and Hunt producing a number of watercolours of the Lizard and surrounding coast. Since they regarded this as a holiday it can be assumed the sketches were made for the artist's own enjoyment and experiment rather than any financial gain. Indeed most of Hunt's work, as well as featuring geological features, seems to involve the study of the dynamics and movement of the sea – new subject matter for him at this time.

Watercolours made by Hunt on this trip include, in addition to the present work, the following:

- an unfinished study *The Lizard* (exhibited: Walker Art Gallery, Liverpool, 1969, no 197)
- *The Land's End, Cornwall*, (reproduced: William Holman Hunt, *Pre-Raphaelitism and the Pre-Raphaelite Brotherhood*, 1905, Vol II, page 157)
- *Helston, Cornwall* (collection: Whitworth Art Gallery, Manchester)
- *Asparagus Island* (exhibited: *The Pictures of Mr. Holman Hunt*, Fine Art Society, 1886, no 30; and *The Pre-Raphaelites*, Tate Gallery, London, 1984, no 232)

At the time that *Cornish Coast* was reproduced (*The Old Water-Colour Society's Club Annual Volume XIII*, 1935-36, plate VIII) it was owned by Mrs Sydney Morse whose husband had been a Kensington solicitor and an important patron of Hunt, so it was presumably purchased directly from the artist. Hunt himself noted in his memoirs that:

> *[Prinsep and I] placed ourselves upon a tongue of cliff which divided a large bight into two smaller bays: thence we could, to right and left, see down to the emerald waves breaking with foam white on to the porphyry rocks* (William Holman Hunt, *Pre-Raphaelitism and the Pre-Raphaelite Brotherhood*, London: Macmillan & Co, 1905, Vol II, page 214)

William Holman Hunt continued to paint with great vitality and vigour until failing eyesight at the age of seventy-seven finished his career. He died on 7 September 1910 and two days later was interred in St Paul's Cathedral. One of the pallbearers was William Michael Rossetti – the only surviving member of the Brotherhood.

Further Reading: Judith Bronkhurst, *William Holman Hunt: A Catalogue Raisonné*, London: Yale University Press, 2004

Biography and notes by Philip Tite

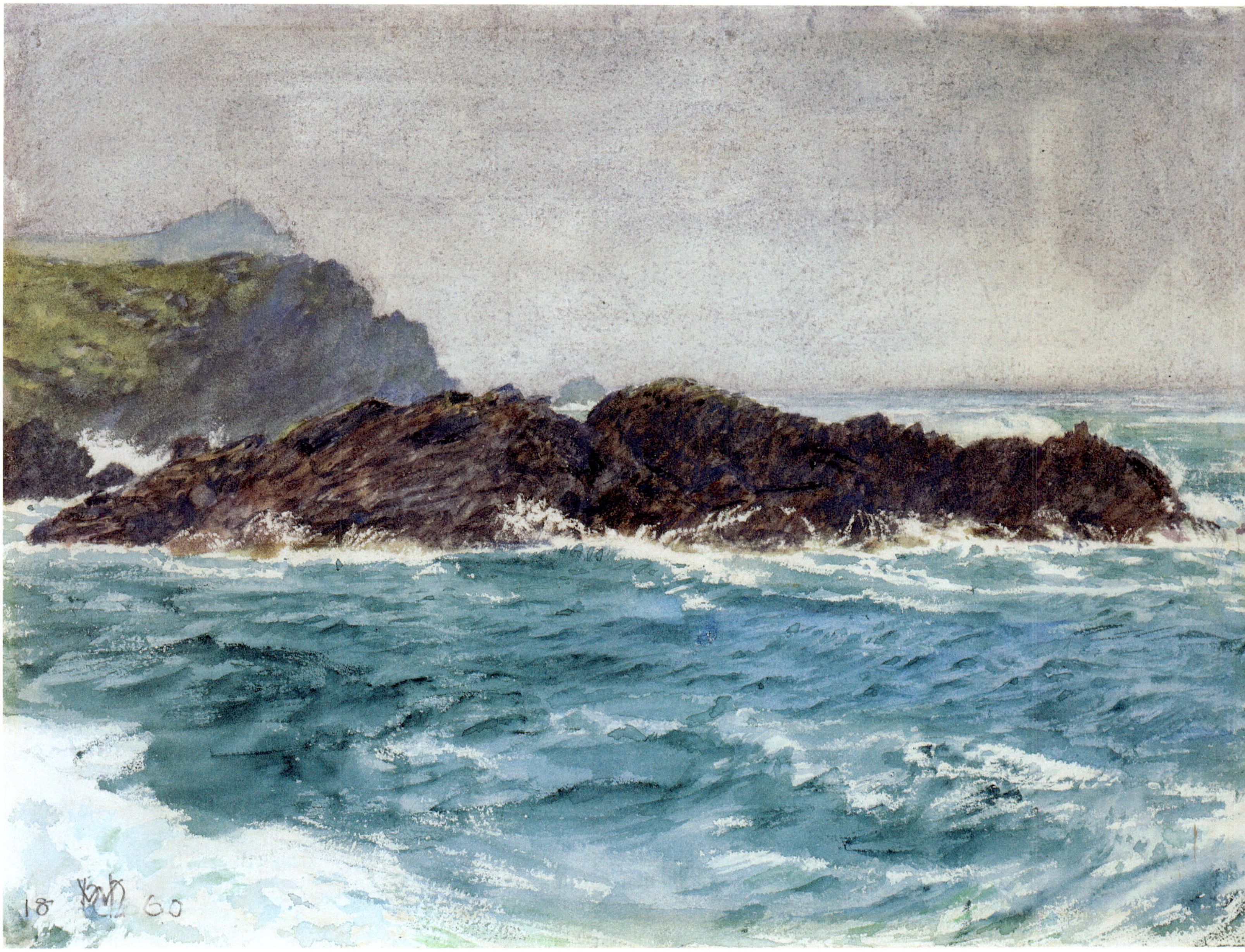

10. Cornish Coast *signed with monogram and dated 1860, watercolour, 7 ¾ x 10 ¼ inches*
Literature; *Old Water-Colour Society's Club Annual Volume XIII*, 1935-36, plate VIII; Judith Bronkhurst, *William Holman Hunt: A Catalogue Raisonné*, London: Yale University Press, 2004, No D200

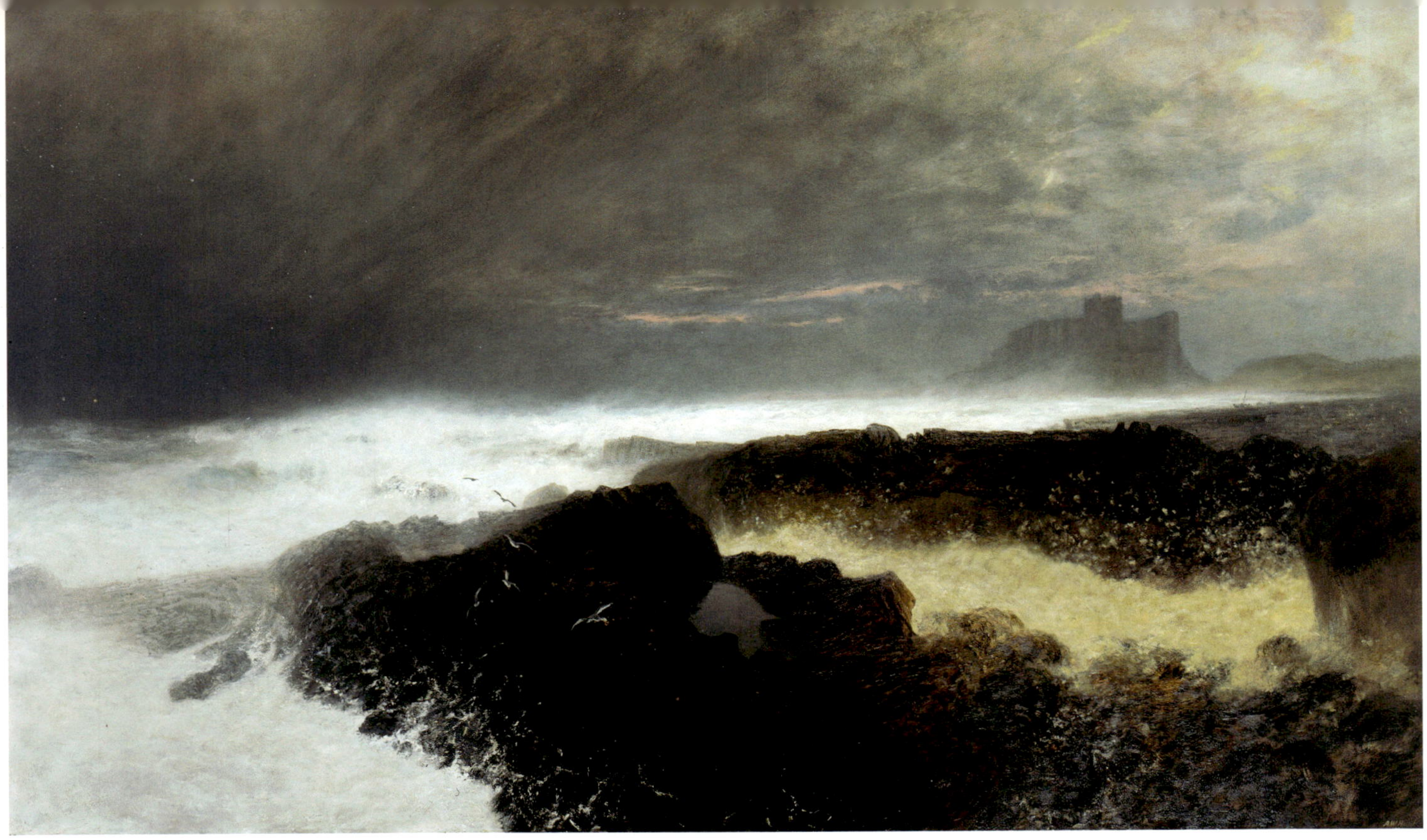

11. Moon Rising over Bamburgh *signed, oil on canvas, 30 x 48 inches*
Exhibited: *Summer Exhibition*, Royal Academy of Arts, 1872, no 1141

Alfred William Hunt

Alfred William Hunt VPRWS (1830–1896)

Alfred William Hunt, like his friend Albert Goodwin, was one of the finest Victorian painters to fully demonstrate the aesthetic of the influential critic John Ruskin. Hunt was born in Liverpool on 15 November 1830, son of the landscape painter, Andrew Hunt. Taking lessons from his father, and absorbing the influence of both his father's friend, David Cox, and J M W Turner, he exhibited from the age of twelve. Blessed with academic and artistic talents, he studied at Oxford (from 1848) with the intention of entering the Church. He won the Newdigate Prize for English Verse (1851) and became a Fellow of Corpus Christi College (1853). For a while he suspended the necessity of taking holy orders, and pursued academic and artistic careers in tandem; he exhibited at the Royal Academy (from 1854) and was elected to the Liverpool Academy (an associate in 1854, and a member two years later).

During this period, Hunt began to read the work of Ruskin, and became so inspired by its aesthetic of 'Truth to Nature' as to develop his art as a synthesis of its Turnerian and Pre-Raphaelite elements. His growing emulation of Turner can clearly be seen in his love of atmospherics, and in the experimental techniques that he employed to achieve them. His loyalty to Pre-Raphaelitism can be understood through the almost scientifically detailed studies he made in preparation for painting. His membership of the Hogarth Club (1858) also demonstrated Pre-Raphaelite affiliations. As a result of these endeavours, he gained and sustained Ruskin's praise, and became his friend and correspondent.

Hunt's dedication to landscape painting also revealed itself in the extensive summer tours that he began to take at this time. He frequently visited the northern counties of England, North Wales and Scotland, and increasingly travelled through Europe.

In 1861, Hunt decided to marry and, in so doing, left the university for Durham, his wife's native town, and devoted himself fully to watercolour painting. A year later he was elected to the Old Water-Colour Society (associate 1862, member 1864), soon becoming a prime mover in raising its status in the art world. On settling in London, in 1865, he took over the Campden Hill studio of the Pre-Raphaelite painter, William Holman Hunt, who was leaving for the Holy Land. He then exhibited mainly at the OWS, where he was properly appreciated by fellow artists and perceptive connoisseurs rather than the general public. He helped engineer the honorary membership of Ruskin to the society (1873) and served as its Vice-President (1880). (The society was renamed the Royal Society of Painters in Water-Colours in 1881). His developing reputation was marked, in 1893, by the inclusion of a group of his works in the World Exhibition in Chicago which he attended. He died in London on 3 May 1896.

Moon Rising over Bamburgh

Alfred William Hunt's patron Robert Stirling Newall – the well-known engineer and astronomer – took a lease on Bamburgh Castle from Lord Crewe in 1871 and Hunt was invited to stay as a guest that same year. He made several watercolours and drawings of Bamburgh in a variety of light and weather conditions, some of which were retained by the Newall family (see *The Newall Collection of English Drawings and Watercolours*, London: Christie's, 13 and 14 December 1979, lots 172-173). A watercolour of Bamburgh Castle taken from exactly the same viewpoint as the present picture was exhibited at the *Coronation Exhibition*, Laing Art Gallery, Newcastle-upon-Tyne, 1953, no 50. However, this picture is the only oil painting of the scene that is known.

Notes by Philip Tite

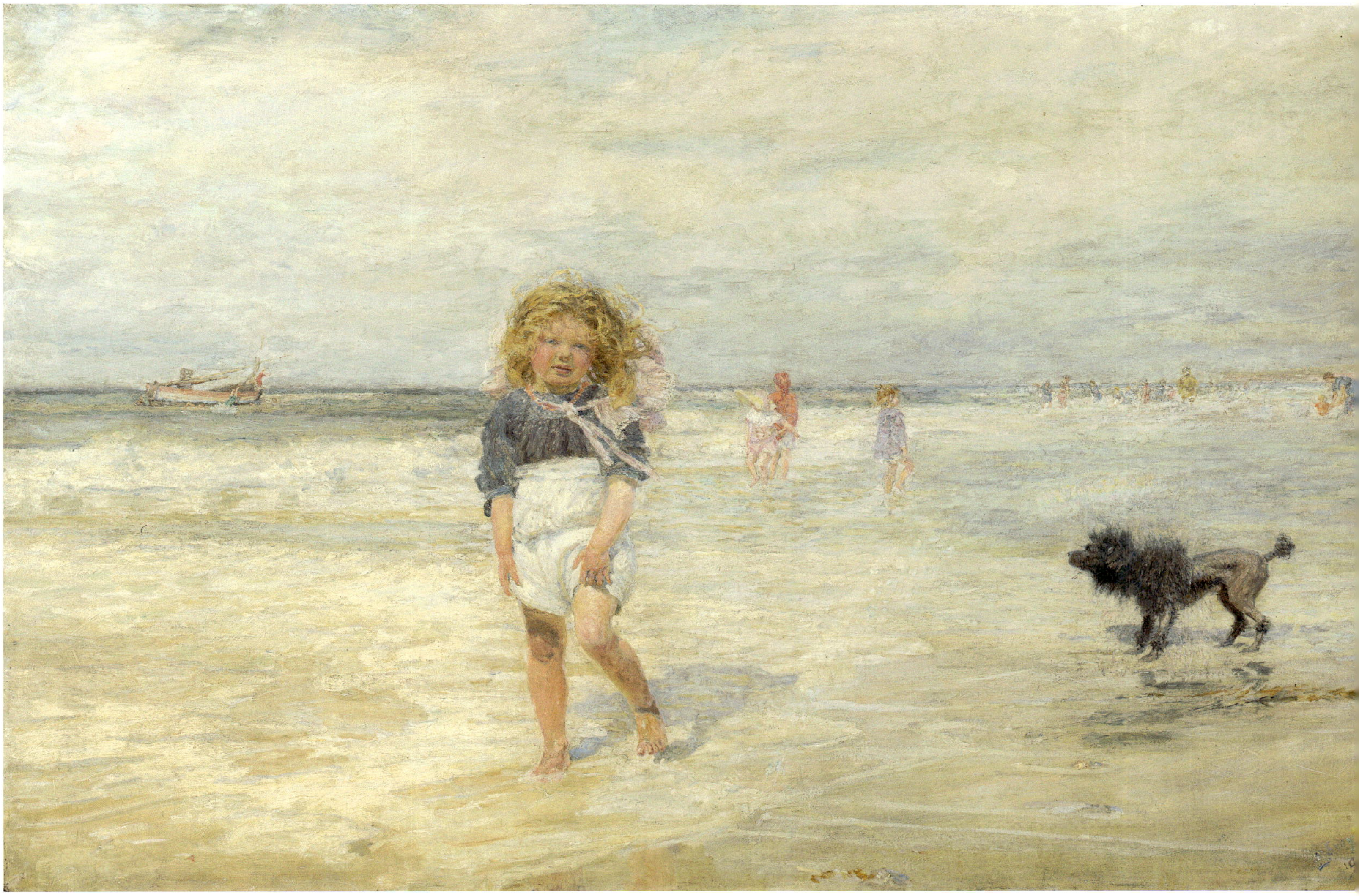

12. Summer *signed and dated 1909, oil on canvas, 32 x 48 inches*
Literature: Rosa M Whitlaw and W L Wyllie, *Lionel P Smythe RA RWS. His Life and Work*, London: Selwyn & Blount, 1923, plate facing page 174 and page 176
Exhibited: *Summer Exhibition*, Royal Academy of Arts, 1907, no 377; Walker Art Gallery, Liverpool, Autumn 1907, no 233

Lionel Percy Smythe

Lionel Percy Smythe RA RI ROI RWS (1839–1918)

The half-brother of W L Wyllie, Lionel Percy Smythe was born on 4 September 1839. He was educated in Paris and in London, at King's College School and Heatherley's School of Art. He was a friend of John William North, and can be associated with him and other English 'Idyllist' painters in his delicate approach to painting. However, he spent much of his life from childhood onwards at Wimereux in Normandy, and he often painted the landscape and life in the area. Between 1879 and 1882, he and his family occupied a Napoleonic fortress on the dunes near Boulogne, a building which was eventually engulfed by the sea. They then moved to the Château d'Honvault, on a hill between Wimereux and Ambleteuse, which then remained their principal home. Smythe had begun to exhibit his work in 1860, at leading London and provincial venues, including the Royal Academy. He was elected to the membership of the Royal Institute of Painters in Water-Colours (1880), the Royal Institute of Painters in Oils (1883), the Royal Society of Painters in Water-Colours (ARWS 1892, RWS 1894) and the Royal Academy (ARA 1898, RA 1911). He died on 10 July 1918.

Further reading: Rosa M Whitlaw and W L Wyllie, *Lionel P Smythe RA RWS: His Life and Work*, London: Selwyn and Blount, 1923

Summer

> *In 1907 he sent* Melting Snows *and* Summer *to the Academy. This last, an oil colour, represented the beach with a good-sized figure of a paddling child in full sunlight, her bare legs shining with salt water; a black poodle at the right of the picture has just come out of the sea and is shaking himself, the flying drops forming a rainbow round him. We were set to work making rainbows with the garden syringe while the picture was in progress.* (Rosa M Whitlaw and W L Wyllie, *Lionel P Smythe RA RWS. His Life and Work*, London: Selwyn & Blount, 1923, page 176)

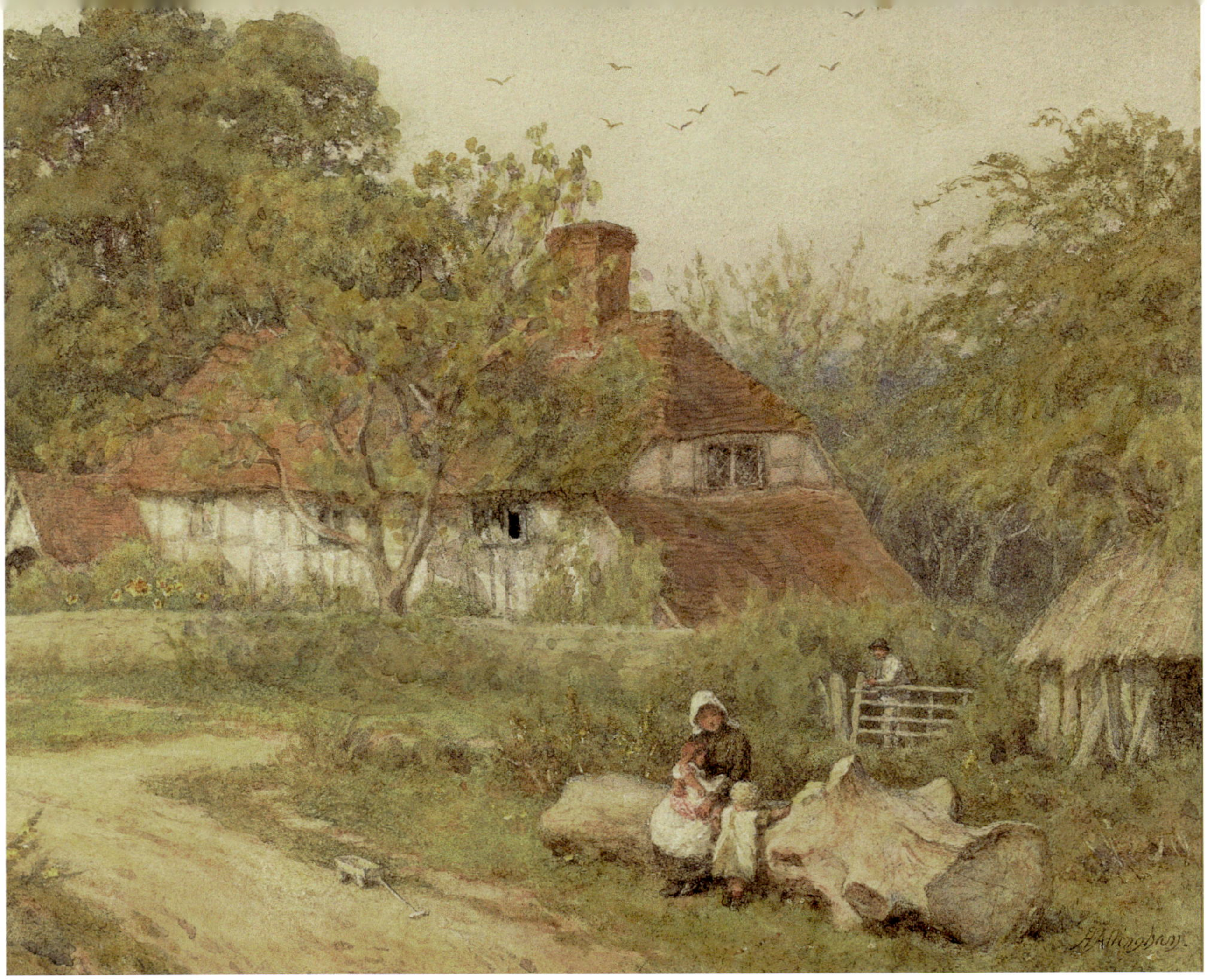

13. The Family Cottage *watercolour, 6 ¾ x 7 ¾ inches*

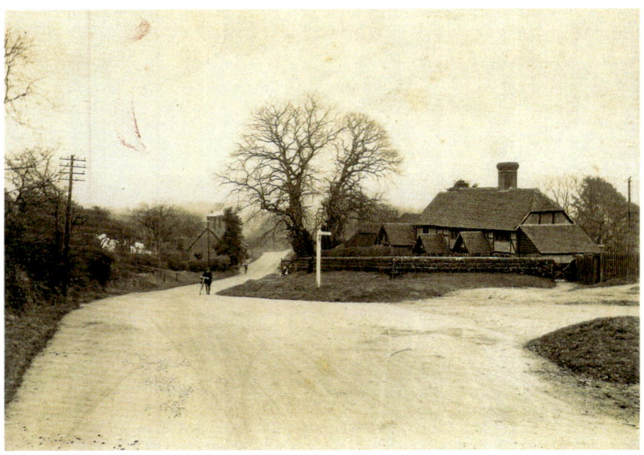

The Family Cottage

The cottage featured in this watercolour has been identified as the one at 61 Petworth Road, Haslemere, Surrey. Now known as *Courts*, it houses the headquarters of the charity, Chernobyl Children Life Line. Allingham worked regularly in Haslemere and the surrounding area from 1880, and would die there in 1926 while visiting her old friend, Mrs Daffurn of Valewood.

With thanks to Annabel Watts for help in compiling this note.

Helen Allingham

Helen Allingham (née Paterson) RWS (1848–1926)

Helen Allingham is the archetypal Victorian painter of cottages and gardens. She was born on 26 September 1848 in Swadlingcote, near Burton-on-Trent, Staffordshire. She studied at the Birmingham School of Design, the South Kensington Schools and the Royal Academy Schools. She began to support herself by drawing illustrations for *Once a Week* and other periodicals, work which led, in 1870, to a permanent position as an artist on the staff of *The Graphic*. In the same year she began to exhibit drawings at the Dudley Gallery. At that time, she was particularly influenced by the work of Fred Walker and Myles Birket Foster, who later became a friend.

Following her marriage to the Irish poet William Allingham, in 1874, she gave up her place on *The Graphic*. However, she continued to produce occasional illustrations for the *Cornhill* magazine and other periodicals and books. Placed by her marriage at the centre of the Cheyne Walk set, she met John Ruskin, who became an admirer of her work. She was, by then, more fully engaged in establishing a career as a watercolourist. She was elected an associate member of the Old Watercolour Society in 1875, and when in 1890 full membership was opened to ladies, she was immediately promoted.

Between 1881 and 1888, Helen Allingham lived in Witley, Surrey, and specialised increasingly in scenes of rural life. These were exhibited in her first two solo shows at the Fine Art Society (1886, 1887). Following her return to London, she continued to make regular sketching expeditions, often in the company of Kate Greenaway. By the late 1890s she was making efforts to expand the range of her subject matter. She died at Haslemere, Surrey on 28 September 1926.

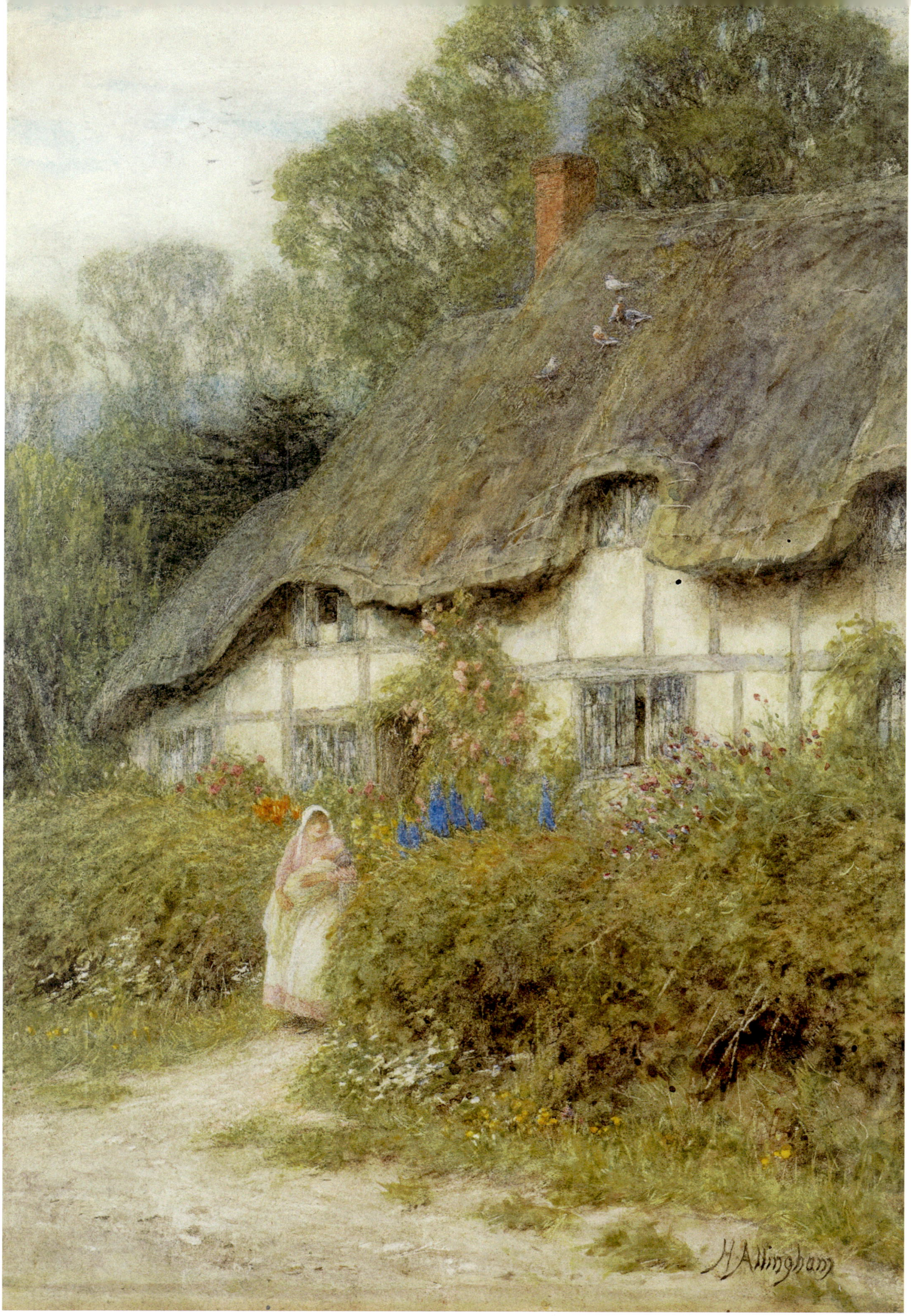

14. A Wiltshire Cottage *signed, inscribed with title on original backboard, watercolour, 10 ¼ x 6 ¾ inches*

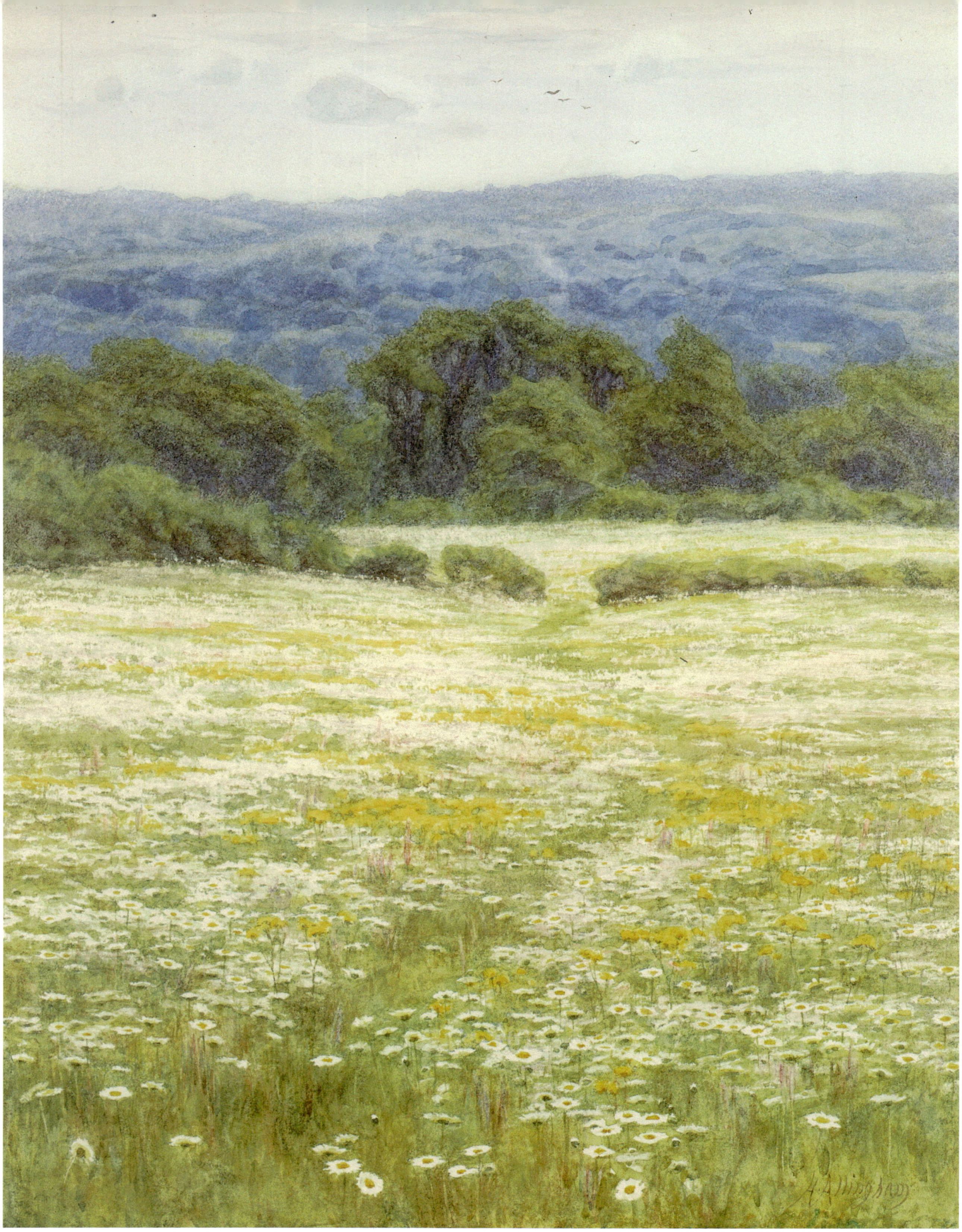

15. Ox-eye Daisies nr Westerham, Kent signed, inscribed with title below mount, watercolour, 10 ¾ x 8 inches
Literature: Marcus B Huish, *Happy England. As painted by Helen Allingham, RWS*, London: A & C Black, 1903, plate 38 and pages 111-113

Ox-eye Daisies nr Westerham, Kent

The drawing was made from the window of the farmhouse in Kent, to which... Mrs Allingham runs down at all seasons. It was evidently made on a glorious summer day, when every flower had expanded to its utmost under the delicious heat of a ripening sun. The bulbous cloudlet which floats in front of the whiter strata, and the blueness of the distant woods may augur rain in the near future, but for the moment everything appears to be in a serenely happy condition, except perhaps the farmer, who would fain see a crop in which there was less flower and more grass. (Marcus B Huish, *Happy England. As painted by Helen Allingham, RWS*, London: A & C Black, 1903, pages 112-113)

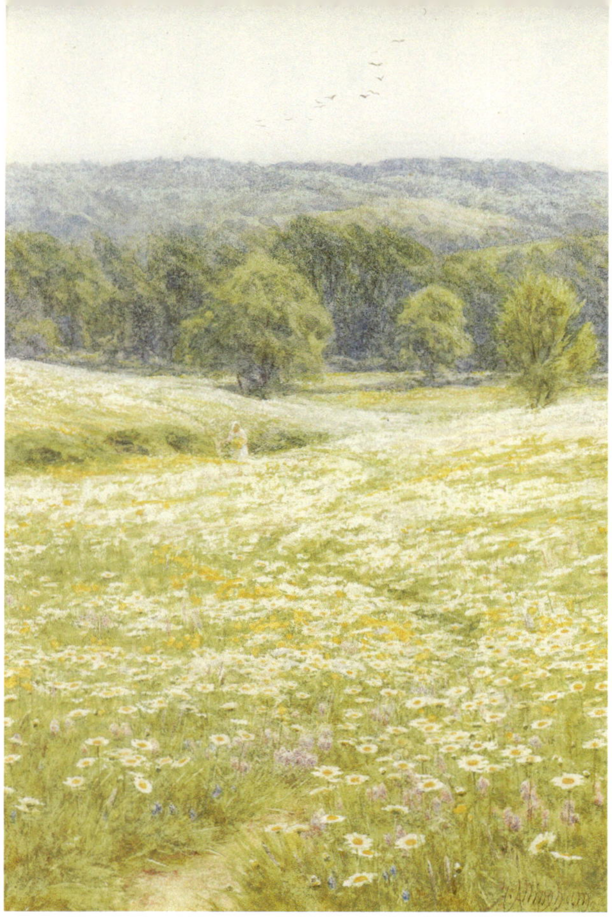

16. Ox-eye Daisies, near Westerham, Kent

signed, inscribed with title on reverse, watercolour, 8 ¼ x 5 ¼ inches

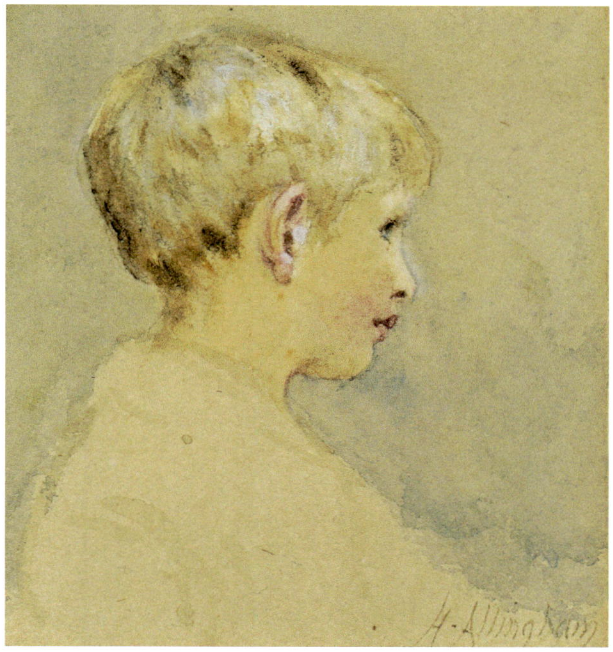

17. Head of a Boy

watercolour, 3 x 2 ¾ inches

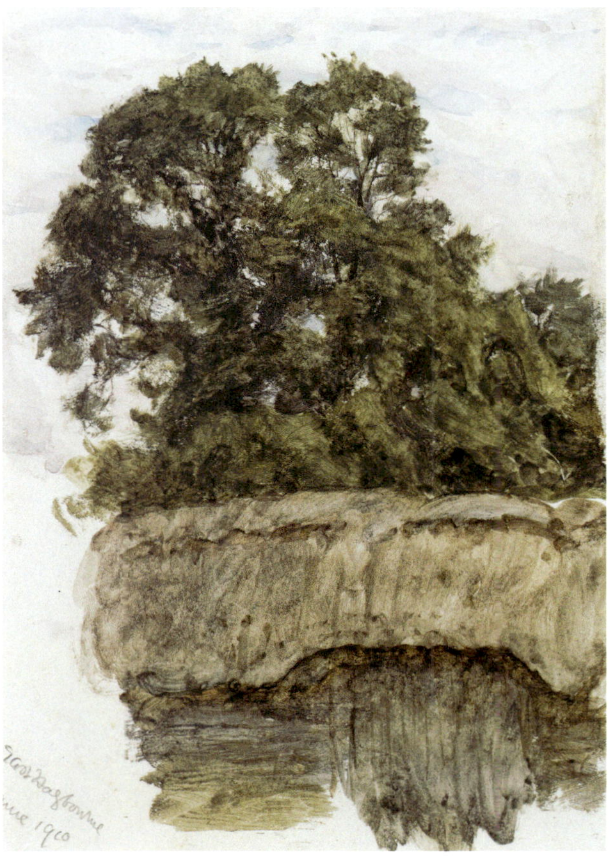

18. At East Hagbourne

inscribed with title and dated June 1910, watercolour, 7 ½ x 5 ¼ inches

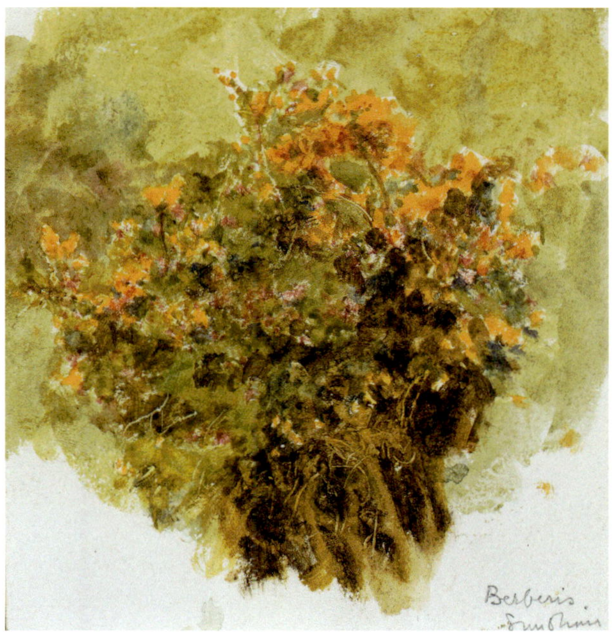

19. Berberis, Sunshine

inscribed with title, watercolour, 4 ¼ x 4 ¼ inches

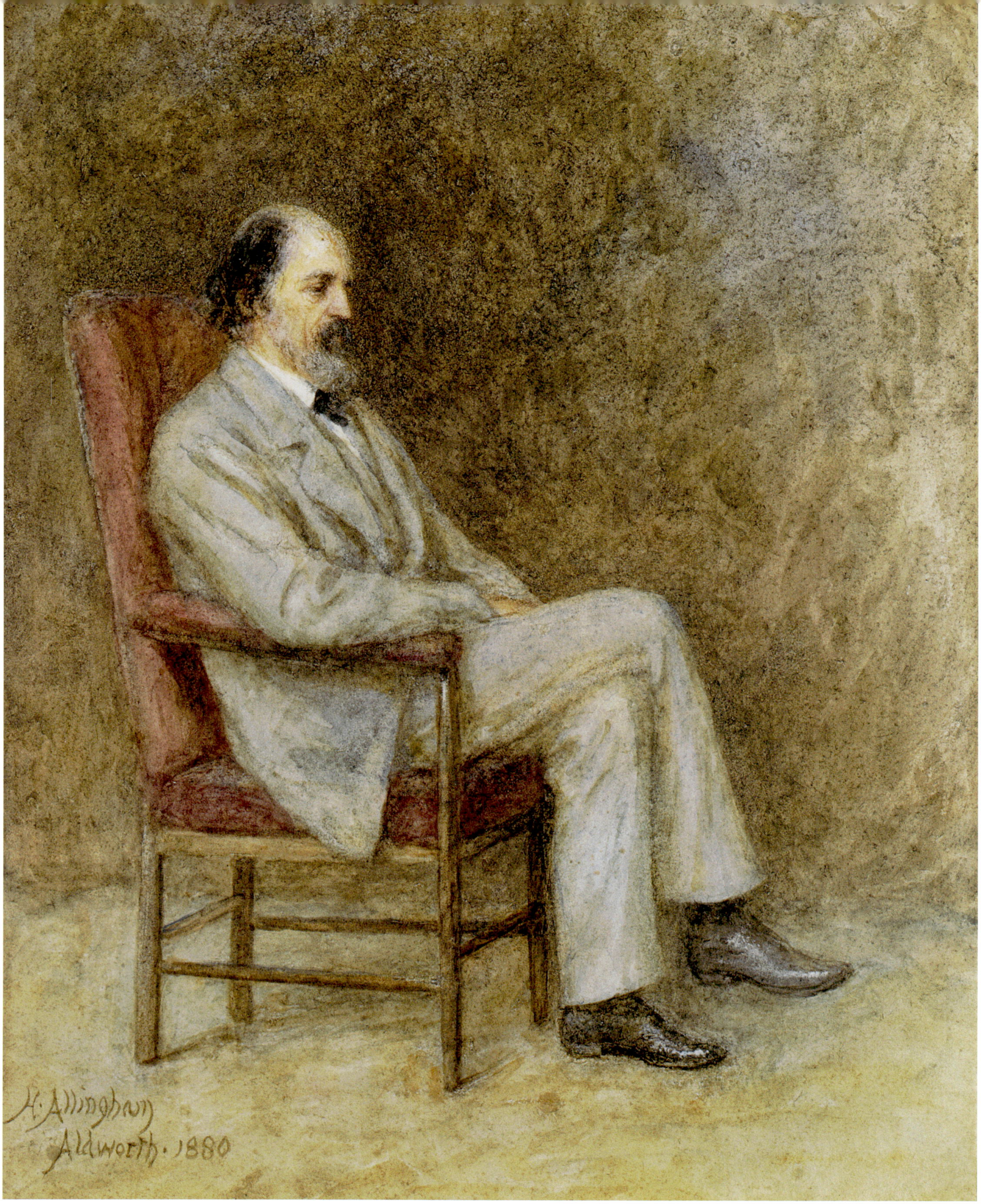

20. Alfred, Lord Tennyson *signed and dated 'Aldworth 1880'*
watercolour, 7 ½ X 6 inches

Alfred, Lord Tennyson

> *[Helen Allingham] is the only person who has made a successful portrait of me though many have tried* (Thomas Carlyle)

In 1853, the young Irish writer, William Allingham sent his first volume of verse to his idol, Alfred, Lord Tennyson, the Poet Laureate. He received, in response, an invitation to call on Tennyson and, in accepting, made the first of frequent visits. These developed into such a close friendship that one of Tennyson's biographers has written that 'Allingham was like an adopted son to him' (Peter Levi, *Tennyson*, London: Macmillan, 1993, page 268).

By the time that Helen Paterson became Mrs William Allingham in 1874, her husband was the author of the popular *Up the Airy Mountain* and a member of a significant literary circle. They lived first in Trafalgar Square, Chelsea, to be near Thomas Carlyle; then, following that writer's death in 1881, they moved to Witley, Surrey, a village close to Tennyson's summer home at Aldworth, over the border in Sussex.

Aldworth had been built in 1868-69, to designs by James Knowles after sketches by Tennyson himself. The landscape that surrounds it is very different from that around the poet's existing house at Freshwater, on the Isle of Wight. The Allinghams made their first visit there on 5 August 1880, while they were staying in Haslemere. Their arrival is described in William's diary, a vital source of information on Tennyson:

> *Walked through the house, long hall open at each end, and found tea on the further lawn, smooth, shut in with shrubs... A T in sombrero and gray suit, broad shouldered. He has been at Venice, Cadore, etc, with Hallam [his son].* (*William Allingham's Diary 1847-1889*, London: Centaur Press, 2000, pages 286-287)

Throughout the summer, indeed until October, the Allinghams returned to Aldworth on numerous occasions. Tennyson encouraged Helen to paint the views from the house, and William's diary entries suggest that, while she worked during the long afternoons, the men conversed about literature.

Tennyson initially refused to have Helen paint his portrait, saying 'I'll go out of the door if you keep looking at me' and 'you're staring at me. He's keeping me in talk. It's a plot. I hate it' (words recorded by Charles Tennyson in his biography of his grandfather, London: Macmillan, 1949, page 451). On 13 October, however, she came up with a successful ruse, as described by William in his diary:

> *Helen, at [Tennyson's] wish, made a sketch of the landscape as seen through one of the arches of the porch. T, looking over her, said: 'I suppose I owe you £20 for this?' H said the payment would be to give her a sitting or two, and he gave in rather grumblingly...*
> *H had two or three short sittings in his study, with fading light, and made a couple of beginnings. He promised to sit again when we next met. I talked to him while he sat, and tried to keep from looking unhappy.* (op cit, pages 301-302)

Given that the date of the present work is 'Aldworth 1880', and that Tennyson is wearing that 'gray suit', it is almost certainly the finished work that resulted from these sittings, and the first of the very few portraits that Helen produced of Tennyson. Tennyson's response contrasts with that of Carlyle, who had happily sat for a dozen of the artist's watercolours, and had said to William that, 'Your wife is the *only* person who has made a successful portrait of me though many have tried' (6 November 1878). Helen Allingham's accomplishment as a painter of literary portraits has been somewhat overshadowed by her great and popular skill of depicting country life and landscapes.

Over the years, Helen developed a friendship with Tennyson, which was independent of William, and continued after William's death in 1889. In the autumn of 1881, for instance, she visited Aldworth alone. After lunch,

> *the Poet accompanied her [to paint at Fox's Holes], and as there were no chairs available for the artist, helped her to arrange bundles of pea-sticks for seats, saying as he sat down beside her: 'I should like to paint. It does not look very difficult,' – with a smile, – 'it must be much pleasanter to paint than to write'.* (Arthur Paterson, *The Homes of Tennyson. Painted by Helen Allingham*, London: A & C Black, 1905, page 84)

Much later, he would show her some of his own watercolours made from the imagination, and again allowed her to paint him. She was with him just before he died in 1892, and paid tribute to him in 1905 by publishing *The Homes of Tennyson*, with reproductions of her watercolours and a text by her brother. The view *From the Porch, Aldworth* – which Tennyson had suggested, and which sparked the present portrait – is included in that volume.

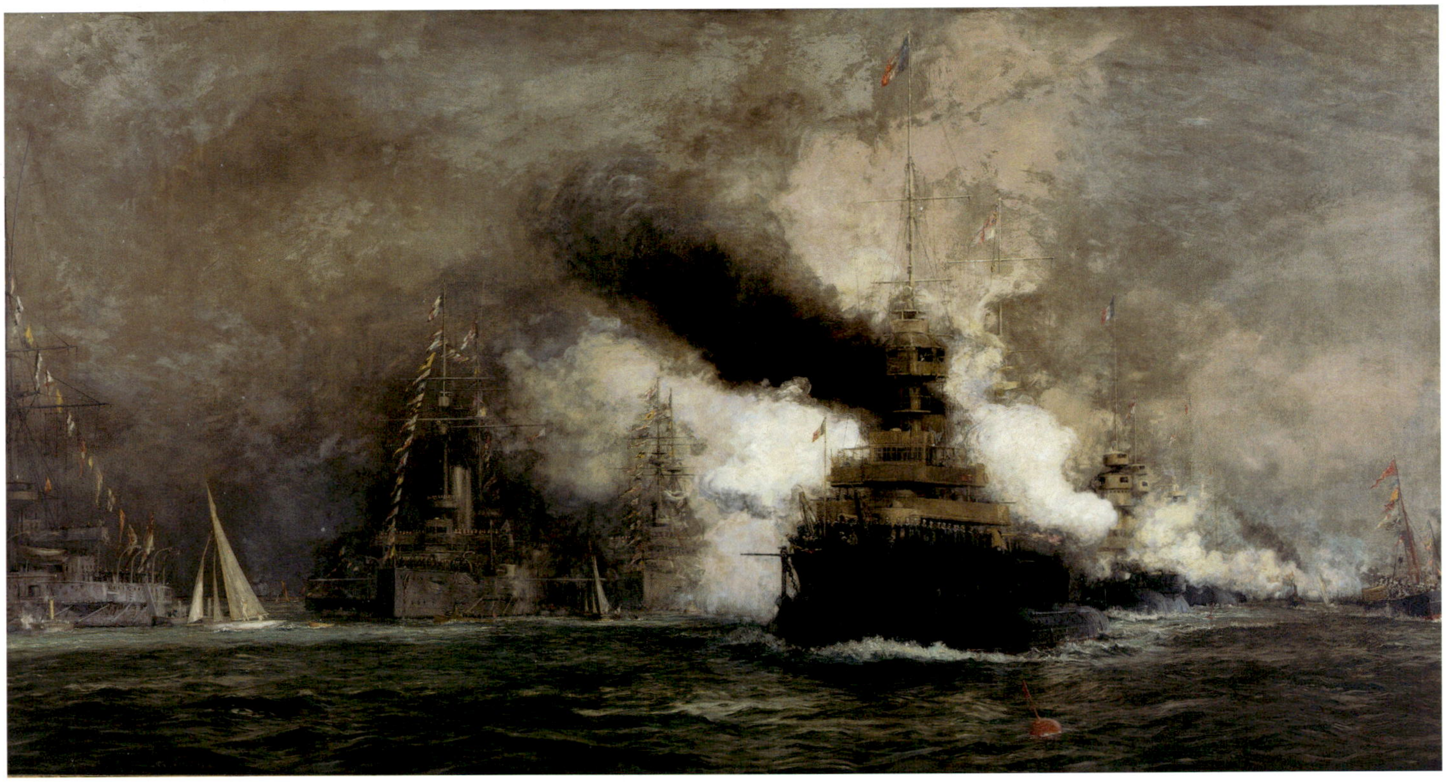

21. L'Entente Cordiale: Arrival of the French Fleet in Cowes Roads *signed and dated 1906, oil on canvas, 60 x 108 inches*
Provenance: Wyllie Memorial Studio, Portsmouth
Literature: M A Wyllie, *We Were One. A Life of W L Wyllie*, London: G Bell, 1935, plate facing page 184, pages 184-186
Exhibited: Summer Exhibition, Royal Academy of Arts, 1906, no 442; *W L Wyllie and L'Entente Cordiale*, Chris Beetles Ltd, June-July 1988

William Lionel Wyllie

William Lionel Wyllie RA RBA RE RI NEAC (1851-1931)

William Lionel Wyllie was born in London on 5 July 1851, son of the painter William Morrison Wyllie. As a child, he lived in Albany Street, close to Regent's Park, and spent summers at Wimereux, on the French coast, where he began to sketch, encouraged by his father and his half-brother, Lionel Percy Smythe. He studied art at Heatherley's (1865) and at the Royal Academy Schools (1866-69), where he won the Turner Medal in his final year. He also made a study of the history of shipbuilding to help him with his paintings. He was influenced by Henry Moore, Whistler and Turner, of whom he later wrote a study (1905).

Wyllie worked initially as a marine illustrator for *The Graphic* (1870-90), and from 1883 produced etchings for Robert Dunthorne of the Rembrandt Gallery. In 1884, he published *Tidal Thames*, the first of a number of books that he both wrote and illustrated. Exhibiting at such leading London venues as the Royal Academy, he had five solo shows at the Fine Art Society (from 1883). He was elected to the Society of British Artists (1875); the New English Art Club (1887); the Royal Institute of Painters in Water-Colours (1882, resigning in 1884, but being re-elected in 1917); a Royal Academician (ARA 1889, RA 1907); to the Royal Society of Painter-Etchers and Engravers (ARE 1903, RE 1904).

In 1884, Wyllie moved to Gillingham House, near Chatham, settling shortly after at Hoo St Werburgh. He then formed a close association with the Royal Navy, which he sealed, in 1907, on moving to Portsmouth, where he lived in the Tower House. He was Marine Painter to the Royal Yacht Squadron and the Royal Victoria Yacht Club, and did much work, including posters, for the Orient Company, White Star Line and Union Castle Line. Often sailing in the barge *Ladybird* and in yachts, he made painting trips to Holland and Northern France. In 1917 he painted an aerial view of the Battle of Bourlon Wood, for which Air Marshal Trenchard sent maps and aerial photographs. Between 1924 and 1930 he worked on a Panorama of Trafalgar for the Victory Museum, Portsmouth. He died in London on 6 April 1931.

Further reading: Roger Quarm and J Wyllie, *W L Wyllie: Marine Artist, 1851-1931*, London: Chris Beetles Ltd, 1981

L'Entente Cordiale

> *The picture is before me as I write. It is the strongest picture that he ever painted. The Entente Cordiale at that moment was complete. God grant it may be so again.* (M A Wyllie, *We Were One. A Life of W L Wyllie*, London: G Bell, 1935, page 185)

At the turn of the nineteenth century, Britain was facing deep hostility from all her European neighbours. The policy of Splendid Isolation, which had seen Britain disassociating herself from

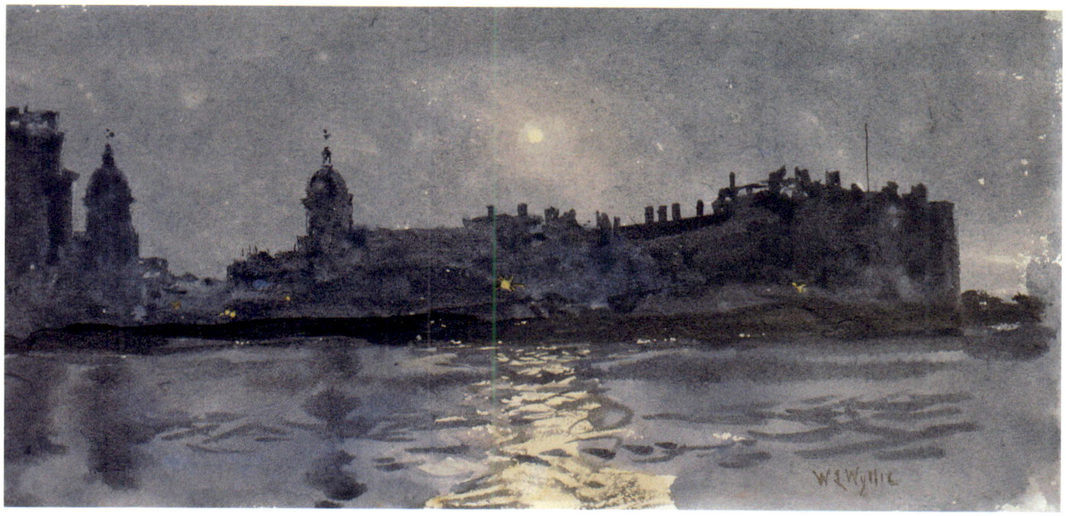

22. Greenwich
signed, watercolour
3 ¾ x 7 ¼ inches

formal alliances between the major European powers, no longer seemed viable as her Empire came increasingly under threat from the imperial aspirations of France, Germany, Austria and Russia. It had always been felt that, as the strongest global power, Britain did not need any defensive aid nor did she want to be dragged into unnecessary wars to defend any one else's borders. However, after the Boer War (1899-1902), it became particularly apparent that by separating her interests from those of the rest of Europe, Britain was in danger of goading central powers in Europe into putting aside their own quarrels and uniting against her. Most disturbingly, there was growing evidence that Germany, a supposed ally, was designing a navy to rival Britain's impressive fleet. For Britain this could only mean that Germany was preparing for future combat with the British, as possible disputes with France and Russia could only ever be settled on land.

The result of these growing fears was the restoration of the traditional entente with France. For Britain this would mean support against German threats to her imperial interests, and the settling of several colonial disputes with France ranging from Siam to Madagascar and West Africa to Newfoundland. The crux of the agreement was a French acceptance of British control of Egypt in return for British recognition of French predominance in Morocco. The agreement was made on 8 April 1904 and marked the end of Britain's Splendid Isolation in Europe. It was however, still seen only as a friendly agreement; an *Entente Cordiale* rather than a formal alliance. Its purpose was to dispel Anglo-French tension so that neither country need be reliant on Germany in a crisis. It was not intended to be an alliance against Germany. Nevertheless, by 1905, a series of German challenges to the *Entente* had already taken place so that, as Wyllie painted the present picture, the *Entente* was transforming into an alliance and the diplomatic tensions in Europe were preparing the British for the idea of war with Germany.

In the biography of her husband, *We Were One*, Marian Wyllie described the scene of the painting, when the French fleet came into the English channel early in August 1905, as part of the celebrations to mark the signing of the *Entente Cordiale*:

It is not often that one has the privilege of seeing the sight that Bill and I, in company with thousands, witnessed that day in the summer of 1905 when the French fleet came to England and the Entente Cordiale was complete. Our French brothers were with us, and it was a real joy that filled the souls on board the union Castle liner Armadale Castle.

As the splendid French squadron came in view, the weather that had been wet and cold cleared – just as a faint ghost of the ships was sighted on the horizon, the thick clouds dispersed. On the squadron came, bringing the sunlight with them from La Belle France pushing from their bows the big white waves of misunderstanding and prejudice as they approached through a band of pale brilliant green sea. Led by the Masséna and keeping perfect station, on they came, belching thick black smoke that hid the hulls of the ships in the rear from sight, only allowing the tall Marconi masts, with their bright waving tricolours to appear above it.

As the flagship came abreast of the Armadale Castle, a ringing cheer burst out, which the Frenchmen returned with interest. The excursion boats heeled sponsors under, with their shouting mass of humanity taking up the tale. The fleet with its virile workman-like torpedo boats steamed majestically up the Solent. Our splendid Channel fleet of battleships and cruisers dressed with countless fluttering flags and the crews standing with linked hands all round the ships and the tops, was moored in a line from the West Brambles buoy to Off-Brown down point with the destroyers in an inner line to the North and the 1st Cruiser Squadron outside to the south ward.

Off Osbourne, the Masséna broke out a signal which ran down the whole French Line, the ships bursting into flame and white smoke as the guns roared a salute, which was at once answered from the welcoming English fleet…

We steamed ahead slowly and let go anchor at the head of all with a view looking down the double line of brilliantly lighted battleships. A marvellous sight! About 10 o'clock the fireworks began – the most wonderful I verily believe that were ever seen. The ships were not only outlined, but missiles of fire filled the dark skies and searchlights crossed and re-crossed high in the heaven at one moment, then sweeping along the battleships, picking out every detail at the next.

When all was over, the heavens opened, the rain came down in torrents and with thunder and lightning, the Almighty showed man what He could do in comparison to his feeble efforts! (op cit, pages184-186)

Notes by Edwina Freeman

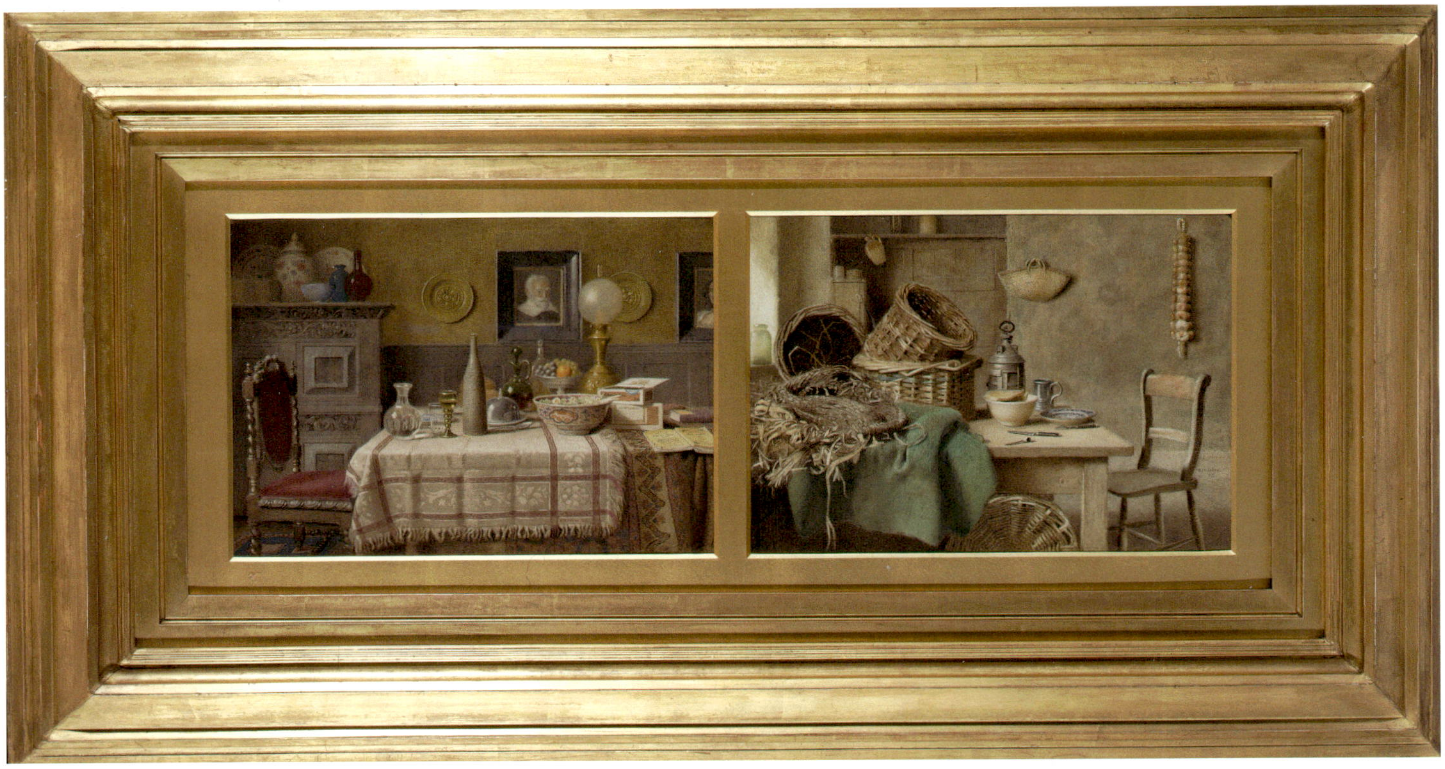

23. High Life and Low Life
signed and inscribed with title on labels on backboard, watercolour, two images each measuring 8 ¾ x 12 ¼ inches
Exhibited: *Summer Exhibition*, Royal Academy of Arts, 1887, nos 1217 and 1218

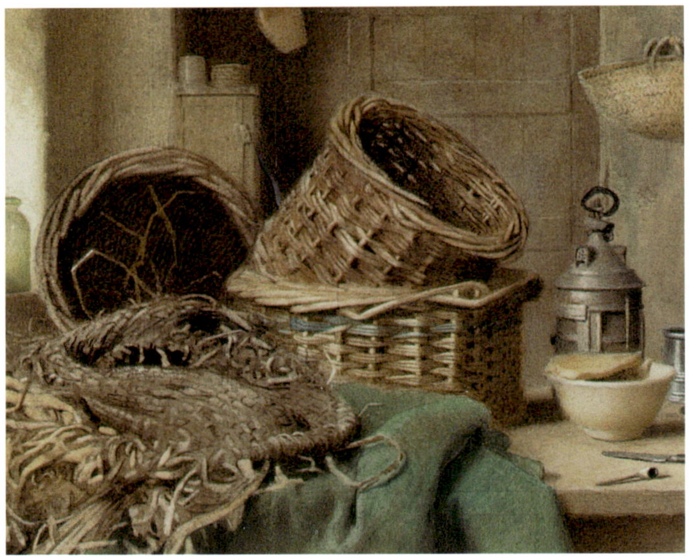

Benjamin Walter Spiers

Benjamin Walter Spiers (active 1875–1893)

Benjamin Walter Spiers packed every corner of his still-life watercolours with objects which test a skill for mimetic detail and reveal an antiquarian turn of mind. Some of his compositions actually show the interiors of his favourite antique shops in Wardour Street, in London's Soho, while one of his pieces may even depict a room in his own Bayswater home. Certainly the frequency with which he reused objects suggests that he owned them or could access them quickly and regularly. Spiers painted in contrary to the type of still life recently established by William Henry Hunt, commended by Ruskin, and here illustrated by the work of John Sherrin, in which nature is represented modestly, and in miniature, by a bird's nest, a mossy bank and a few nuts, fruit or flowers. He may stand as the leading Victorian exponent of another, much more established, still-life tradition of displaying accumulated man-made possessions with almost *trompe l'oeil* accuracy. However, his cluttered collections of battered, mismatched objects often seem to undermine the usual intention of such displays to confirm the wealth of conspicuous consumers. They concentrate not on monetary worth, but on associative value.

Further reading: Christopher Wood, 'Knicknacks and Silly Old Books', *Country Life*, 10 June 1993, pages 124-125

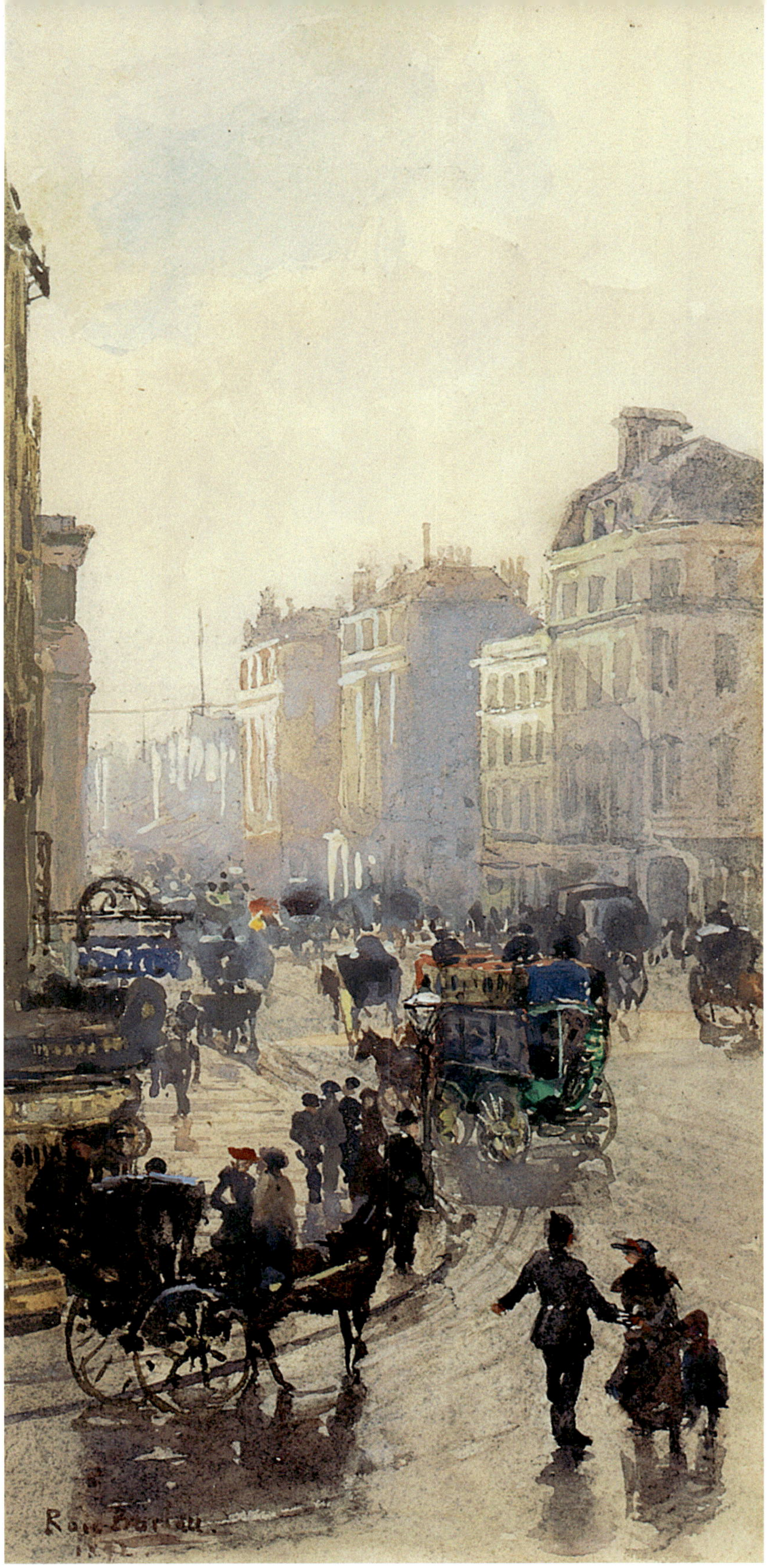

24. Oxford Street from the corner of Bond Street
signed and dated 1892, watercolour, 11 ¾ x 5 ½ inches
Literature: Rose Barton, *Familiar London*, London: A & C Black, 1904, plate 10, facing page 28

Rose Barton

Rose Barton RWS ASWA (1856–1929)

Rose Barton was appreciated even by her contemporaries as the equal of Herbert Menzies Marshall in her work as an urban topographer. She was born in Dublin on 21 April 1856, into a wealthy Anglo-Irish family. Her father was a solicitor in Rochetown, County Tipperary. She was educated privately and studied art first in Brussels (1874), and then alongside her friend Mildred Anne Butler in Paris (under Henri Gervex) and London (under Paul Naftel). She returned to work in Dublin, and began to exhibit widely, both in Ireland (from 1878) and in mainland Britain. Her first important show was that at the Japanese Gallery, in London in 1893, which she shared with George Haité. Five years later, she had a solo show at the Clifford Gallery. Before her permanent move to London in 1903, when she settled in Knightsbridge, she had already been elected an associate of both the Society of Women Artists (1886) and the Royal Society of Painters in Water-Colours (1893; full member 1911). She was also a committee member of the Irish Watercolour Society. She had also proved that her watercolours could be adapted to publication, for she had illustrated *Picturesque Dublin Old and New* (1898). Her work for the publisher A & C Black comprised Familiar London (1904), *The Ramparts of Empire* (illustrated with Norman Wilkinson in 1910) and contributions to *London* (1915). She died at her Knightsbridge home on 10 October 1929.

Further reading: *Rose Barton RWS* (1856-1929), London: Christie's, 1987

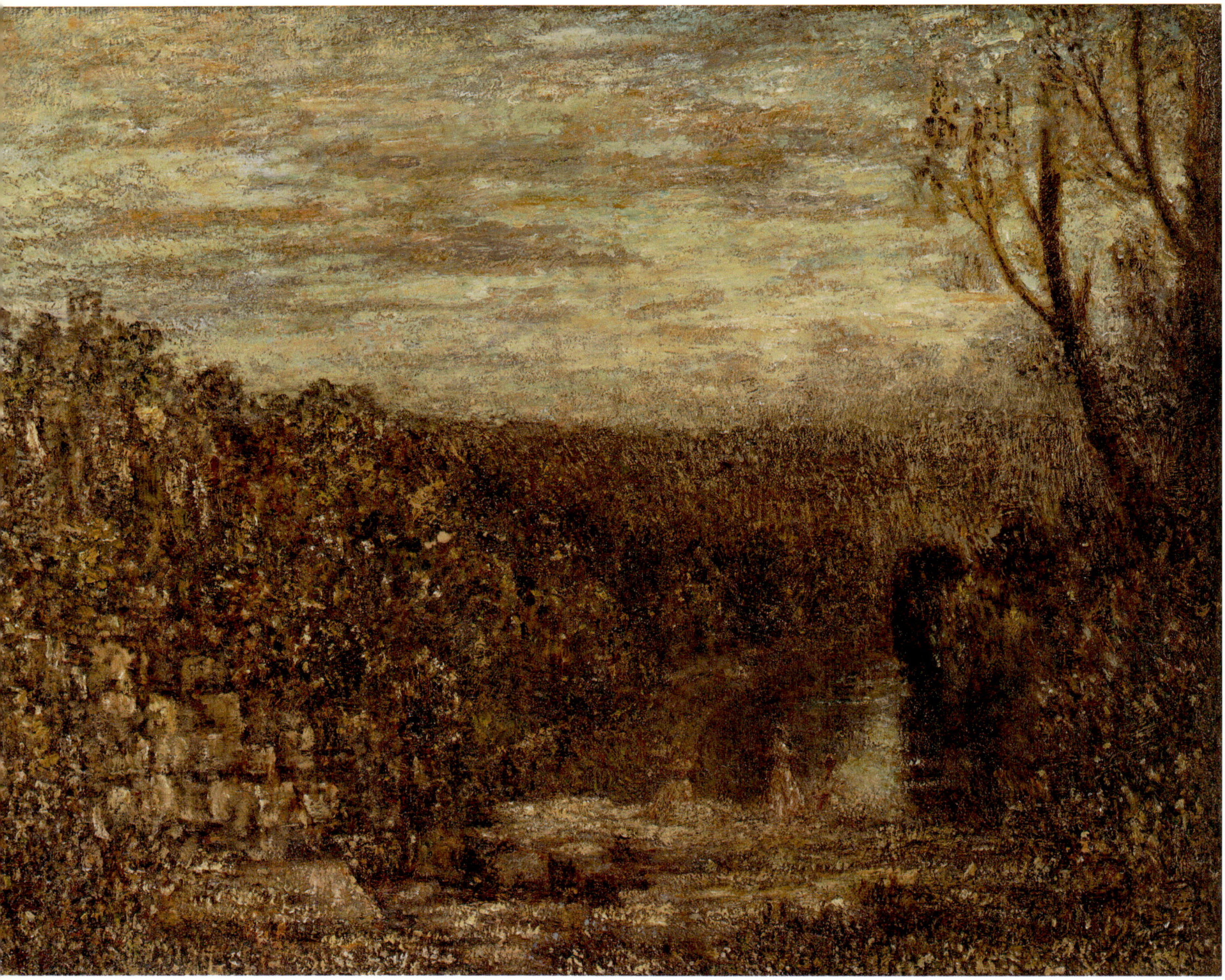

25. A View at Ludlow *oil on canvas, 40 x 50 inches*
Provenance: Sale of Steer's effects, Christie Manson & Woods, 16-17 July 1942, no 124; Lessore; Lord Molson
Literature: D S MacColl, *Life work and setting of Philip Wilson Steer* (with a full catalogue of paintings... by Alfred Yockney), London: Faber & Faber, 1945, page 216; Bruce Laughton, *Philip Wilson Steer 1860-1942*, Oxford: Clarendon Press, 1971, catalogue no 234a and plate 170, as *A view at Ludlow, with three figures in the foreground*
Exhibited: *An Exhibition of Recent and Earlier Works by P Wilson Steer*, Goupil Gallery, March-April 1924, No 68; and/or *Modern British Art*, Goupil Gallery, Summer 1924, no 24 as *The Teme at Ludlow, Sunset* (Priced £350)
Painted circa 1898-99, it was possibly not completed until 1914.

Philip Wilson Steer

Philip Wilson Steer OM NEAC (1860-1942)

Wilson Steer was one of the most interesting British painters working at the turn of the century, his career subsuming early experimentation within a developing traditionalism. The son of a painter, he was born in Birkenhead, Cheshire on 28 December 1860. When the family moved to Whitchurch, Herefordshire four years later, he was educated in Hereford. He studied art at the Gloucester School of Art (1878-80), and the South Kensington Schools (1881), before moving to Paris to study under Bouguereau at the Académie Julian (1882-83), and under Cabanel at the Ecole des Beaux-Arts (1883-84).

In his early days, Steer was influenced by such avant-garde figures as James McNeill Whistler and the French Impressionists. As his submissions to the Royal Academy were skied or rejected (in the period 1883-85), he helped found the New English Art Club (1886) with artists of a similarly innovative character, and also sold work through dealers. Exhibitions of his seaside views at such venues as the Goupil Gallery (solo show, 1894) were particularly helpful in developing his reputation as a figure of great originality. In turn, he conveyed his approach to art to the younger generation through his teaching at the Slade School.

However, at the turn of the century, Steer began to react to his growing success by looking to the more established native tradition of landscape painting, as represented by John Constable and J M W Turner. He painted an increasing number of pure landscapes, working in England, North Wales and sometimes France, and favouring river and coastal scenes. Owing to his failing eyesight he turned increasingly to watercolour and mastered the medium before the end of the First World War. In 1918, he produced a number of watercolours of the manoeuvres of the British Fleet as an Official War Artist. In the post-war period, he was given a major retrospective at the Tate Gallery (1929) and was awarded the Order of Merit (1931). A number of memorial shows followed his death in London on 21 March 1942.

Further reading: Bruce Laughton, *Philip Wilson Steer 1860-1942*, Oxford: Clarendon Press, 1971; D S MacColl, *Life Work and Setting of Philip Wilson Steer*, London: Faber and Faber, 1945

A View at Ludlow

> *Severn and Wye have, time out of mind, been holy ground for English poetry*
> (D S MacColl, *Life Work and Setting of Philip Wilson Steer*, London: Faber & Faber, 1945, page 81)

By the turn of the century, Philip Wilson Steer was busy rehearsing the established native tradition of landscape painting. Following in the footsteps of J M W Turner, he explored Yorkshire and then the Welsh borders – including the valleys of the Severn, Teme and Wye. Turner's sketchbooks reveal that he had worked in Ludlow, on the Teme, in 1798, and Steer first arrived there exactly a century later.

Yet, despite this homage, many of Steer's paintings of Ludlow reveal the influence of another, Continental and more contemporary, artist. The isolated French Romantic painter, Adolphe Monticelli (1824-86), was very fashionable in London at the turn of the century, and especially for his unusual technique and chromatic palette, which together had anticipated aspects of Impressionism and other later trends. For instance, D S MacColl, the leading critic and champion of Steer, praised Monticelli's 'gem-like' encrustations. Bruce Laughton has written that 'what Steer took from Monticelli was the notion of thick paint, as a substance which could be used as an equivalent for visual sensation' (*Philip Wilson Steer 1860-1942*, Oxford: Clarendon Press, 1971, page 87).

When Steer set about producing *A View at Ludlow*, he clearly had Monticelli's technique in mind, as he had three works by the artist in his own collection. While he based the composition on his earlier *Cliffs by the Teme, Ludlow*, he rejected its fluid treatment in favour of a rich impasted handling, and achieved it through a combination of brush, brush handle and palette knife

According to Laughton, 'There were basically two different views from the bank of the River Teme that interested Steer, one looking into a left-hand bend and the other into a right-hand bend' (op cit, page 94). The recurring motif of a small forked tree suggests to Laughton that Steer concentrated on the right-hand view over a period of two years, 1898-1900. *A View at Ludlow* would seem to be one of the later interpretations, in which the tree has been obscured, and the topography generally distilled. Given that the catalogue raisonné by Alfred Yockney (included in MacColl's monograph) dates the painting to 1914, the artist may have worked on it across three decades, returning to the canvas to build up layers in a loving, almost obsessional fashion. If the approach to painting that Ludlow offered Steer seemed at first both retrospective and immediate, it instead became experimental and drenched in memory.

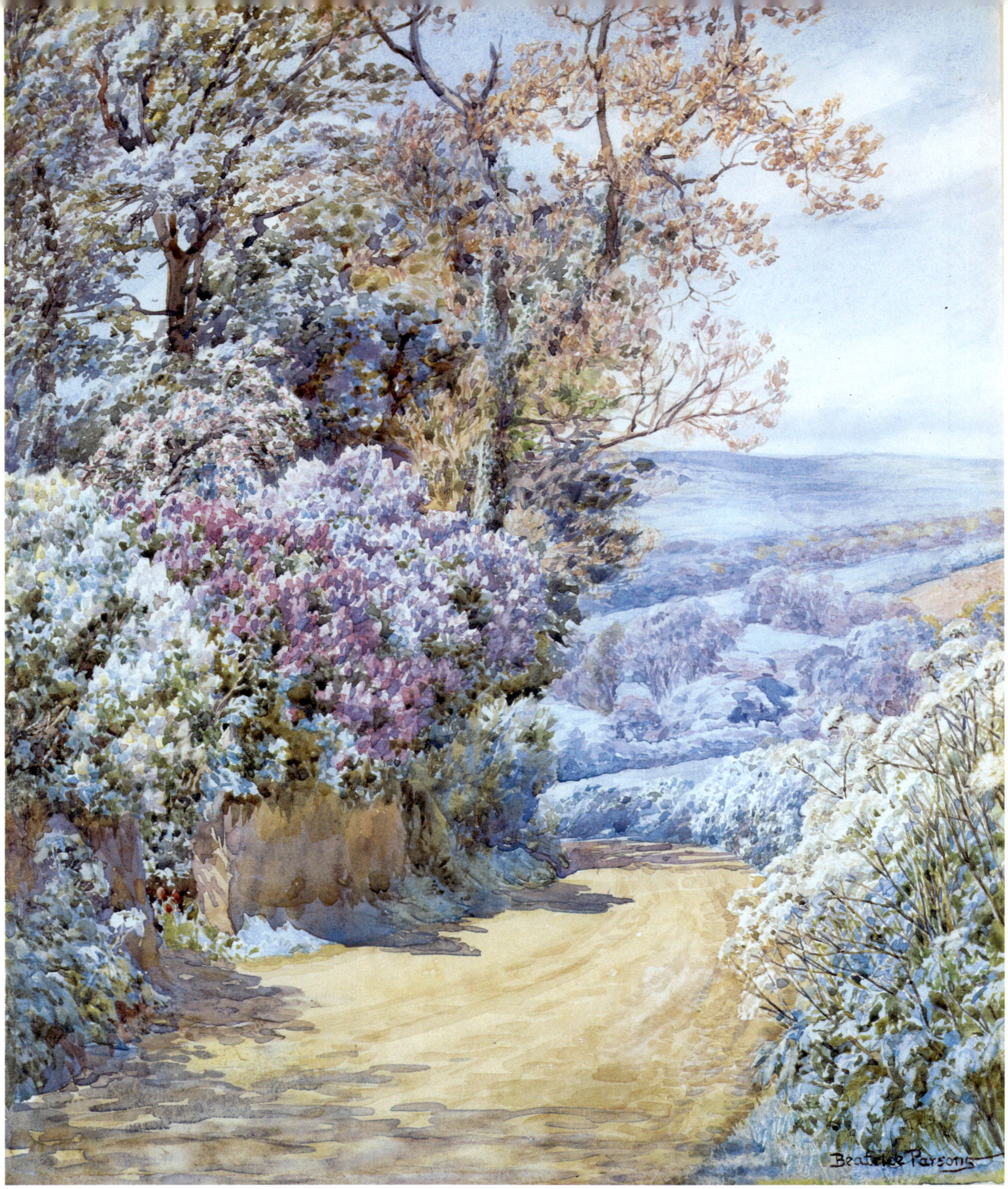

26. Dorset Road in May *inscribed with title and 'No 12' on reverse, signed, watercolour, 12 ¼ x 10 inches*

Beatrice Parsons

Beatrice Emma Parsons (1869-1955)

Beatrice Parsons was the sister of the stained-glass designer Karl Parsons. She was born in Peckham, South London and educated at the Haberdashers' Askes School for Girls, Hatcham, New Cross. She studied drawing under Professor P H Delamotte, at King's College in 1884, and at the Royal Academy Schools, where she won three prizes. Beginning to exhibit at the Royal Academy in 1889, she attempted a variety of subjects but, from the turn of the century, specialised in the detailed depiction of gardens, and especially floral borders. The results were exhibited in some twenty-two highly successful solo shows, mainly at Dowdeswell's Gallery and the Greatorex Gallery, and well over thirty of her works were purchased by Queen Mary, some possibly as commissions. Other notable commissions include those from the Duchess of Westminster and the Duchess of Harewood. She also illustrated a number of books on gardens, including E T Cook's *Gardens of England* (1908) and Dion Clayton Calthrop's *The Charm of Gardens* (1910). She lived in Hampstead (after 1901) and Oxhey, in Hertfordshire (from 1907). She died on 17 February 1955.

Further reading: Diana Baskervyle-Glegg, 'The Painted Garden. The Art of Beatrice Parsons', *Country Life*, 19 March 1987, pages 68-70; Kay Sanecki, 'Painted Under Blue Skies'. *Country Life*, 23 March 1989, pages 180-183

With thanks to Sue Selwyn for help in compiling the biography.

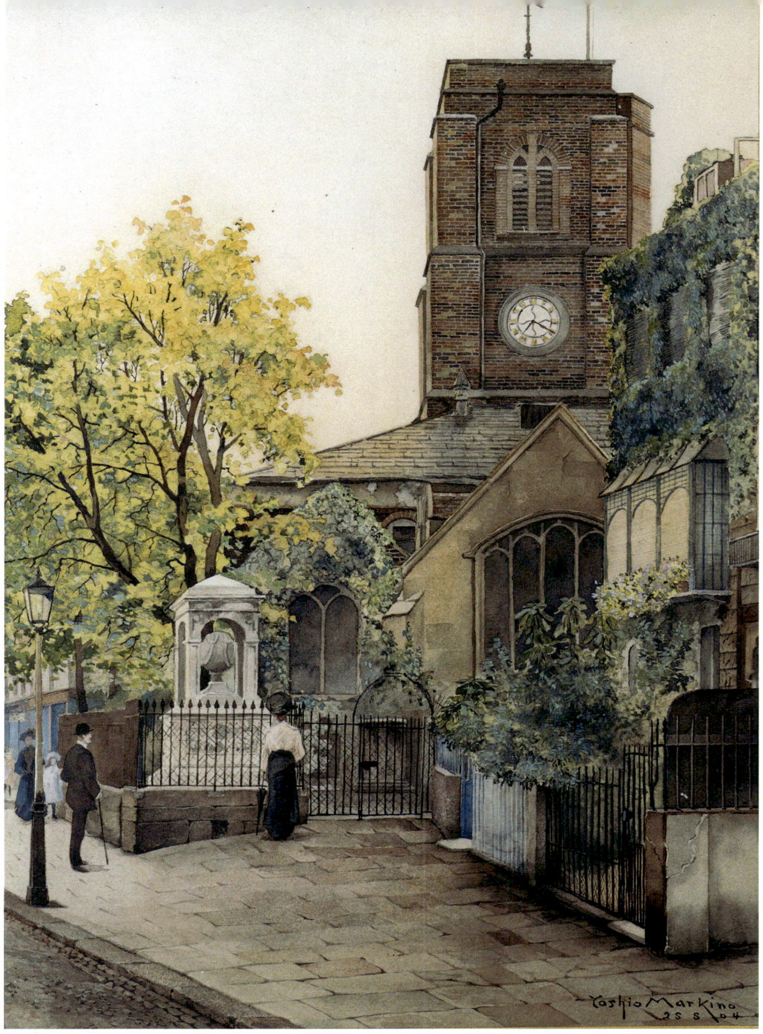

27. Chelsea Old Church *signed and dated '28 8 04', watercolour, 14 ½ x 10 ¼ inches*
Illustrated: Yoshio Markino, *A Japanese Artist in London*, London: Chatto and Windus, 1910, plate 112, as *Chelsea Church*

Chelsea Old Church

Chelsea Old Church was originally the parish church of the village of Chelsea. When painted by Yoshio Markino in 1904, the building comprised the following elements: the Chancel (probably dating from the thirteenth century), the North and South Chapels (about 1325), and the Nave and Tower (1670). The South Chapel, rebuilt by Thomas More in 1528 for his private use, was the part least damaged by a bomb that fell on the church in 1941. All has now been fully restored.

Yoshio Markino

Yoshio Markino, known in Japan as Makino Yoshio (1869-1956)

> *A pleasing 'cross' in aestheticism, a hybrid in artistic practice.*
> (*The Studio*, October 1901, page 58)

Yoshio Markino was born in Koromo, Mikawa, Japan on 25 December 1869. In 1893, at the age of twenty-three, he emigrated to San Francisco, and there attempted to study painting, while enduring poverty and a degree of racial abuse. However, he was treated with greater respect in England, to which he moved in 1897, and so began to feel happier and more secure. It was at this point that he adapted the spelling of his surname from Makino to Markino, so that it would not be pronounced *Maykino*. He gained a position in the office of the Japanese Naval Attaché, made friends among his co-patriots, and took evening classes at the Westminster School of Art. However, this improvement in his fortunes proved short-lived, as he was made redundant from the Naval office. So he entered another period of poverty, which he survived through a combination of his own resilience and the kindness of strangers.

Around the turn of the century, some of Markino's drawings were accepted by M H Spielmann for publication in the *Magazine of Art*. Spielmann introduced the artist to Douglas Sladen, editor of Who's Who, and he became a regular member of Sladen's literary 'At Homes'. Numerous commissions resulted, including one for the illustrations to W J Loftie's *The Colour of London* (1907). The views that he produced for that book synthesised Eastern and Western approaches to picture-making in an original way, and beautifully captured the misty atmospherics of the city; so they made his name and launched him into society. Edmund Dulac, Arthur Waley and Emmeline Pankhurst would eventually be numbered among his many and varied friends. In 1910, he charted the experiences of this period in his illustrated memoir, *A Japanese Artist in London*. The quality of this and other volumes of essays has led Carmen Blacker to write that he 'succeeded Lafcadio Hearn as the chief interpreter of Japan to the Anglo-Saxon nations' ('Yoshio Markino, 1869-1956', 1994, pages 182-183).

Markino was equally successful at interpreting other cities, as is indicated by his illustrations to *The Colour of Paris* by members of the Académie Goncourt (1908), O M Potter's *The Colour of Rome* (1909), and Hugh de Selincourt's *Oxford from Within* (1910). These views were also exhibited in a number of leading London galleries.

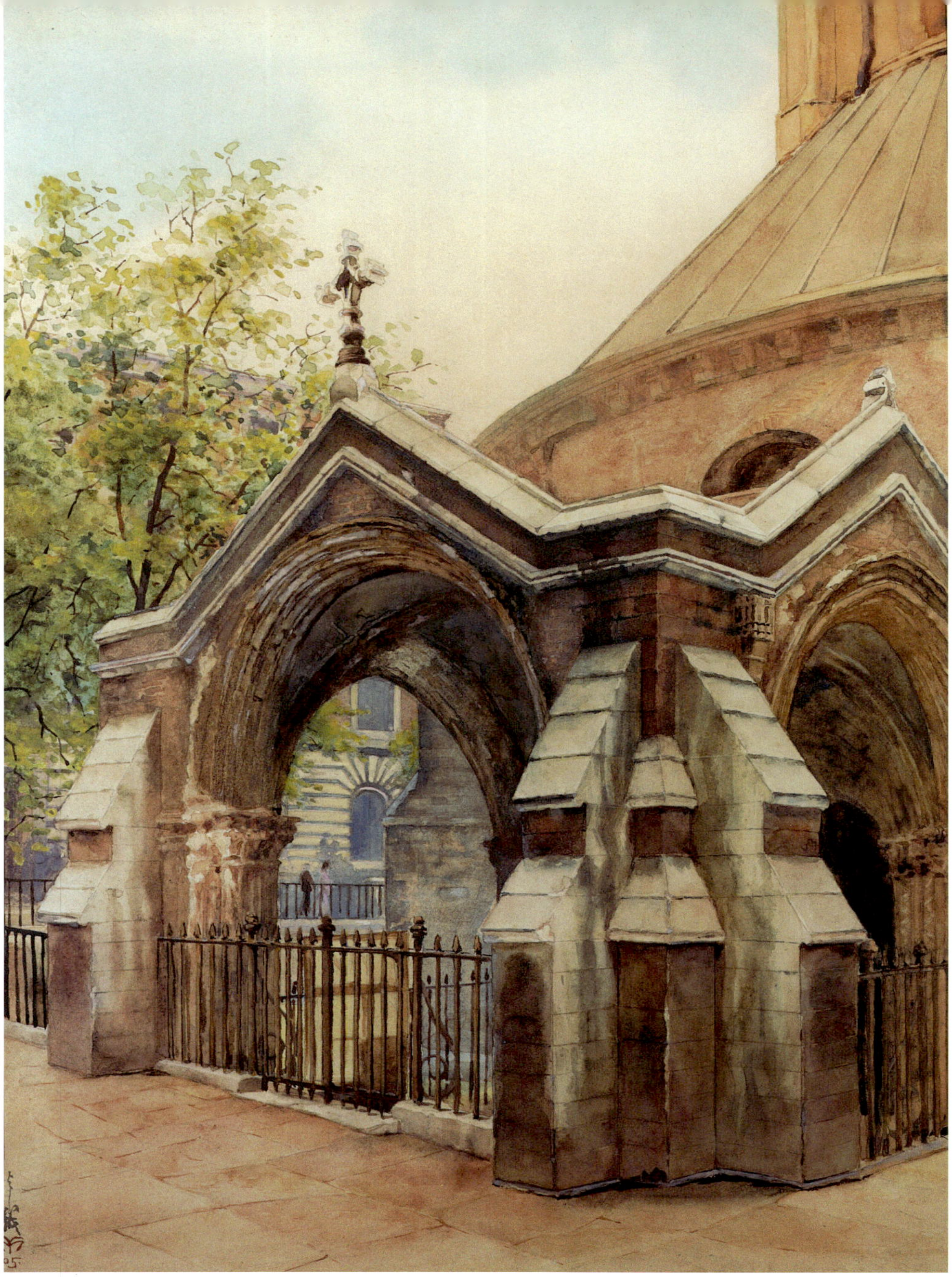

28. The Porch of The Temple Church *signed and dated 05, watercolour, 13 ½ x 9 ¾*

During the First World War, Markino became more retiring, and spent much of his time learning Greek. He subsequently listed 'reading the Ancient Chinese, Latin and Greek classics in order to forget modern civilization' as his recreation in *Who's Who*. When London began to return to its peacetime activities, it seemed to have forgotten Markino, and he relaunched himself, entering into a brief platonic marriage (1922-27) and making a return visit to the United States (1923). Solo shows of the period included *Watercolour Paintings by Yoshio Markino*, at the Art Center, New York (1925) and *America Seen by Yoshio Markino* at the Cottars Studio Gallery, Kensington (1928).

In the late 1930s, Markino befriended the Japanese ambassador, Shigemitsu Mamoru, and, following the outbreak of the Second World War, he moved into a room in the embassy, in Grosvenor Square. Nevertheless, he was repatriated in 1942, and spent the remainder of the war living in poverty in Kamakura, south of Tokyo. In the post-war period, he lived in a little house behind Kitakamakura Station, where he continued to paint. While fostering hopes of returning to England, he died at Akizuki Hospital, Kamakura in October 1956.

Further reading: Carmen Blacker, 'Yoshio Markino, 1869-1956' in Ian Nish (Editor), *Britain & Japan. Biographical Portraits*, Folkstone: Japan Library, 1994, pages 174-189

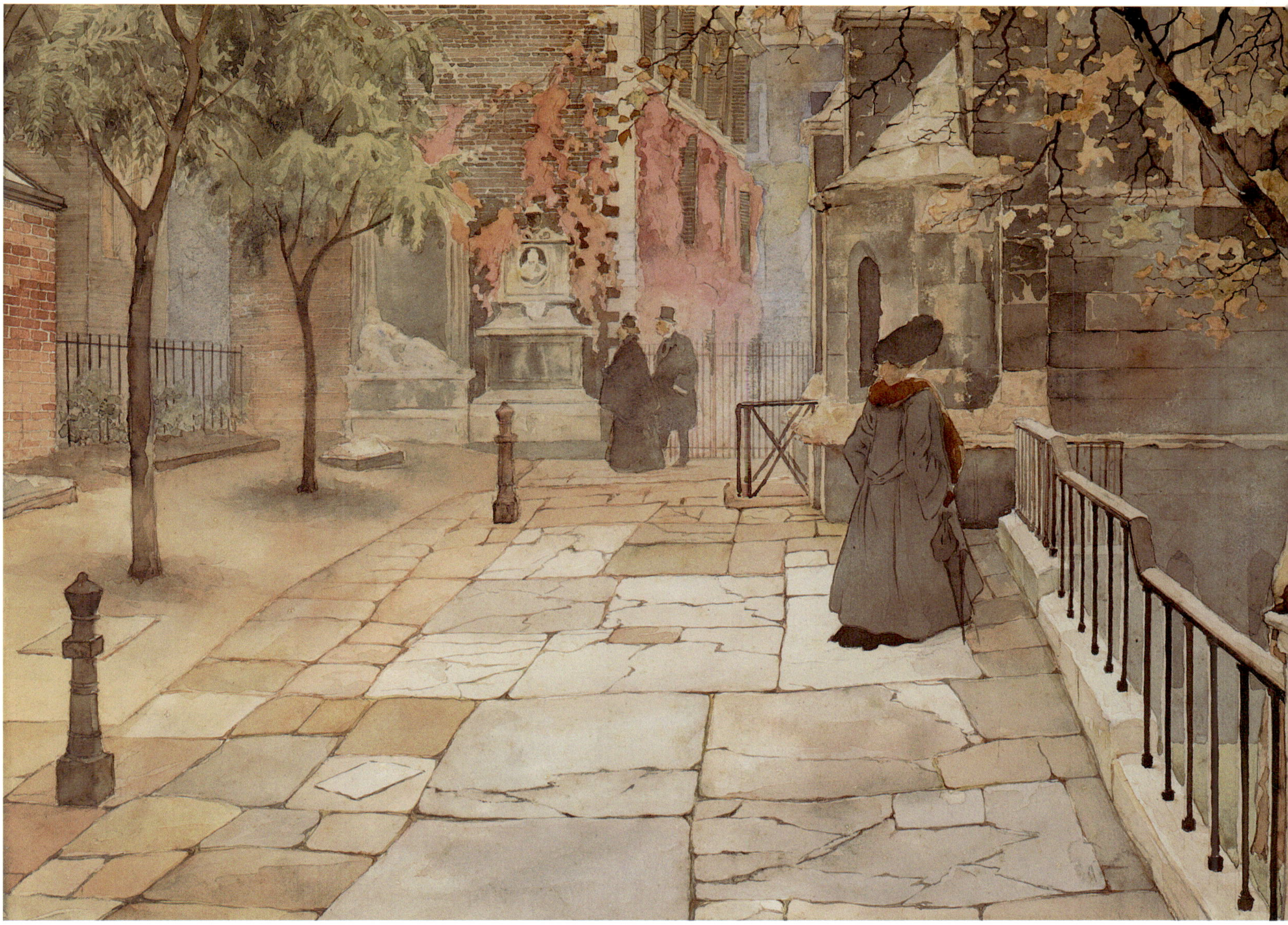

29. Outside The Temple Church *signed with monogram and dated 03, watercolour, 14 x 10 ¼ inches*

The Temple Church

The Temple Church was consecrated on 10 February 1185 as the London headquarters of the Knights Templar. As with all churches of the Templars, it was built on a circular plan in emulation of the Church of the Holy Sepulchre in Jerusalem. In 1240, a rectangular chancel was added with the intention that it would become the resting place of Henry III (though he was eventually buried in Westminster Abbey).

In 1312, Pope Clement V abolished the Knights Templar when the Saracens occupied Jerusalem, making redundant their role of protecting travellers to that city. The Temple Church then went into the control of Edward II, and he gave it to the Knights Hospitaller, who had always worked with the Templars. Subsequently it became the college chapel for the lawyers based in the surrounding Inns of Court. In 1540, Henry VIII abolished the Hospitallers and took control of the church, appointing a Master of the Temple.

Following a royal charter granted to the the Inns of Court by James I, in 1608, they became responsible for the church. Since then the building has undergone a number of restorations, including one in Neo-Gothic style in 1841, and another following bomb damage a century later.

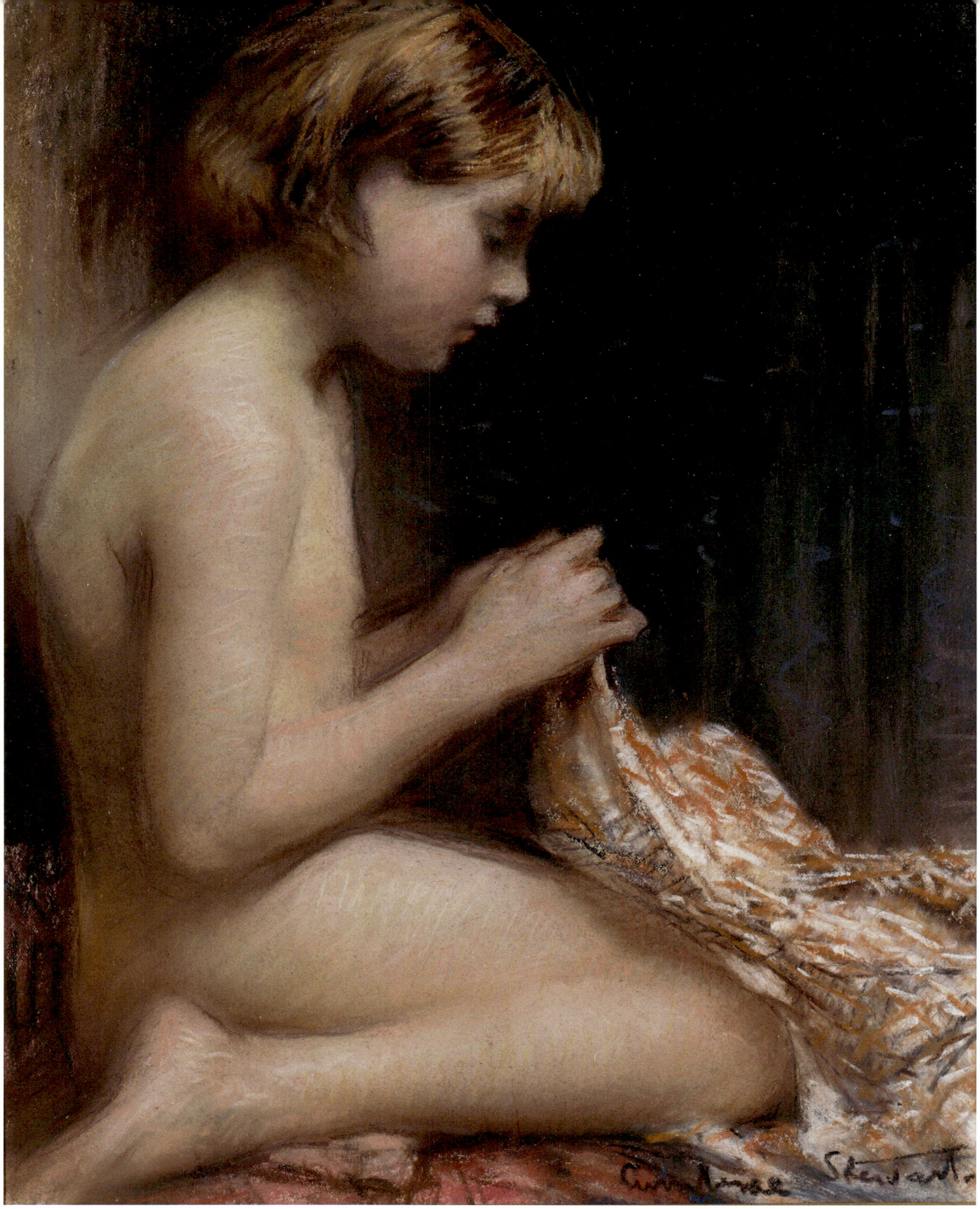

30. Her First Dress *signed, pastel, 13 ¾ x 10 ¾ inches*

Janet Cumbrae Stewart

Janet Agnes Cumbrae Stewart (1883-1960)

Janet Cumbrae Stewart was born on 23 December 1883 in Brighton, near Melbourne, Australia. She studied art with great success in Melbourne, at the National Gallery of Victoria (1901-7), and established herself as a watercolour painter and pastel draughtswoman of landscapes, portraits and figures. In 1915, she won a silver medal at the Panama Pacific Exhibition, in San Francisco. In June 1922, she moved to London and lived on the King's Road, Chelsea. She exhibited her acclaimed pastel studies of nude adults and children at the Royal Academy, the Beaux Arts Gallery and Walker's Gallery, and in the provinces and at the Paris Salon. She later returned to Australia, dying in Melbourne on 8 December 1960.

Further Reading: *Janet Cumbrae Stewart. The Perfect Touch*, Mornington Peninsula Regional Gallery, 2003

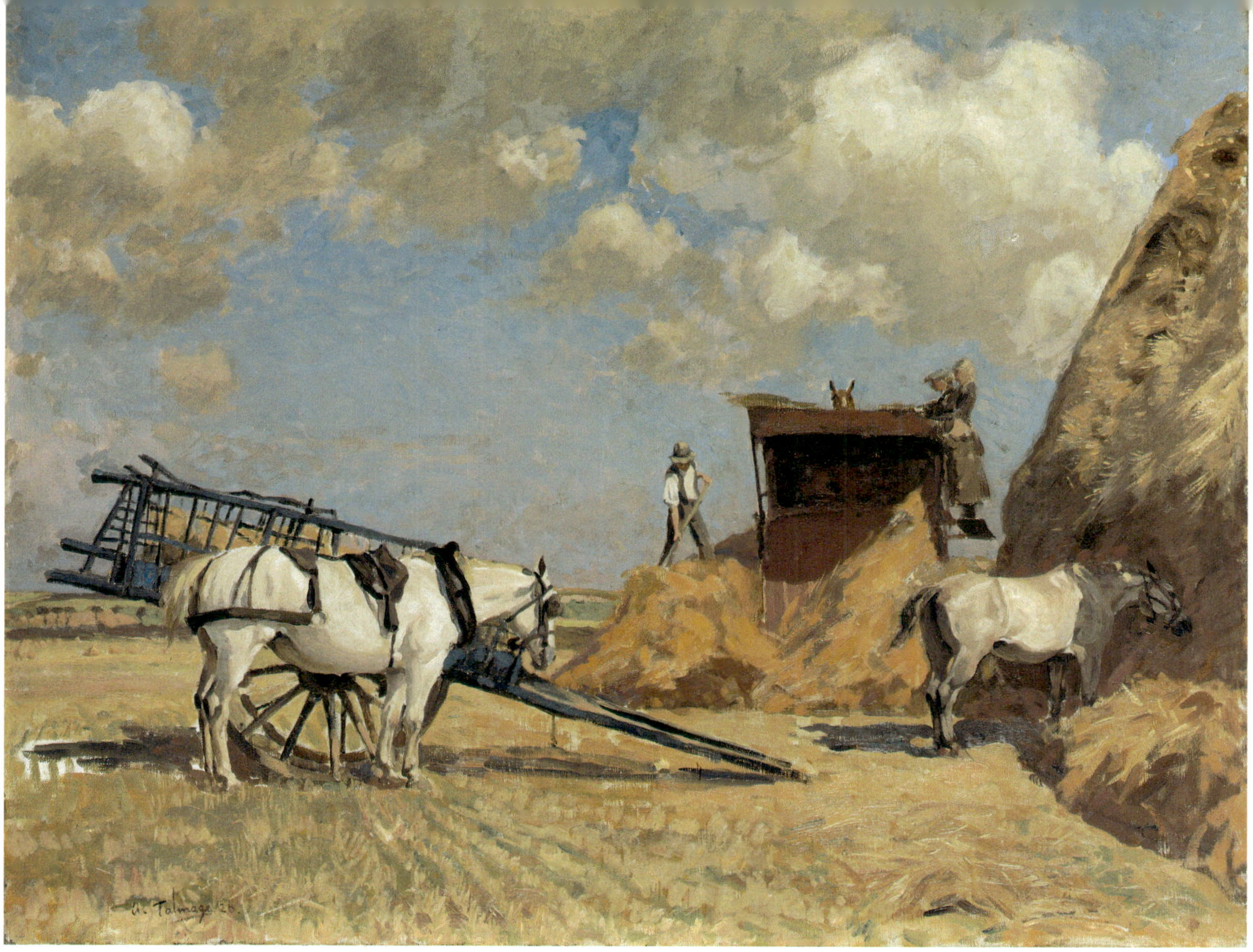

31. A French Harvest *signed and dated 26, oil on canvas, 25 ¾ x 32 inches.* Exhibited: *Summer Exhibition*, Royal Academy of Arts, 1927, no 329

Algernon Talmage

Algernon Mayow Talmage RA ROI RWA (1871-1939)

Algernon Talmage was born in Fifield, Oxfordshire on 23 February 1871, the son of a clergyman. He studied under Sir Hubert von Herkomer at his school of art in Bushey, Hertfordshire. This school, founded in 1883, allowed British artists to pursue an almost Continental training. The students were put to drawing heads from life and from life-casts, and every three months were allowed to try for entry into life classes, which consisted of drawing from nude models. The emphasis on studying from life which Talmage received under Herkomer provided him with the ability to become a versatile painter in the naturalistic tradition.

By 1888, Talmage and two of his fellow students, Arnesby Brown and WHY Titcombe, had discovered in St Ives, Cornwall the familiar security of a small art colony such as they had known in Bushey. Along with such artists as Julius Olsson and Adrian Stokes, Talmage founded an Artist's Club which enabled these painters of the sea to meet and discuss different techniques for capturing the essence of the wild and rugged north coast of Cornwall. By 1900, Talmage and Olsson had established the Cornish School of Landscape, Figure and Sea Painting. The Cornish coastline, made beautiful by the ever-changing light and moods of the sea, enabled Talmage to establish his characteristic mellow palette and enchanting use of light.

For the most part Talmage painted plein-air landscapes and pastorals, and had a passion for painting farming scenes including horses. The later commissions he received from the Canadian Government as an official war artist would allow him to indulge this passion.

Talmage went to London in 1907, and two years later held his first solo show at the Goupil Gallery. He was a regular contributor to the Royal Academy Summer Exhibition, including the exhibition of 1910 which Laura Wortley describes as marking the 'highpoint of "British" Impressionism…which hummed with "air and light"' (*British Impressionism. A Garden of Bright Images*, London: The Studio Fine Art Publications, 1983, page 280). He was elected an Associate of the Royal Academy in 1922, and an Academician seven years later.

The influence of French painting and landscape was important to Talmage. He exhibited successfully at the Paris Salon, winning a silver medal in 1913 and a gold medal in 1922, and travelled to the country on many occasions. He was in Provence from as early as 1894, and possibly in St Tropez as late as 1932. Exhibits at the Royal Academy shown in the same period as the present painting include two paintings of the Pas de Calais.

A French Harvest, dated 1926, perfectly comprises the elements for which Algernon Talmage is most famous, in being a peaceful yet honest scene of rural farming life luminously painted. It also possesses the allegorical quality detected in many of Talmage's post-war paintings, in expressing the new found peace of Britain and France, and the regeneration of the farming communities and the landscape which they worked.

Talmage died near Romsey, Hampshire on 14 September 1939.

Biography by Rebecca Chapman

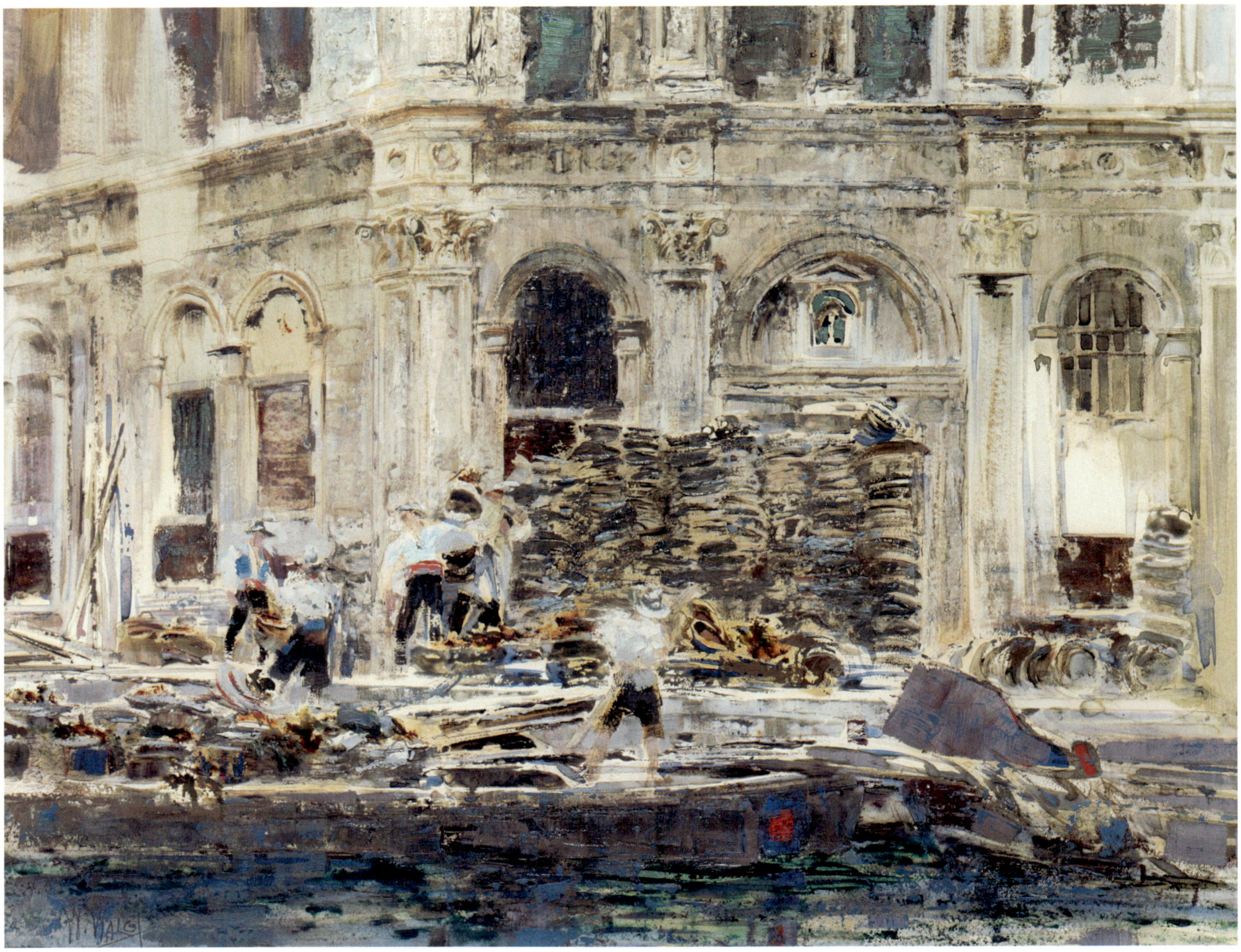

32. Fish Market, Venice *signed, oil on board, 18 ½ x 23 ¼ inches*

William Walcot

William Walcot RBA RE (1874-1943)

The son of an English father and a Russian mother, William Walcot was born at Lustdorf, near Odessa on 10 March 1874. During his childhood, he travelled through Europe with his parents, returning to Russia at the age of seventeen, to study architecture under Alexander Benois at the Imperial Academy of Art, St Petersburg. He also studied in Paris at the Ecole des Beaux-Arts and the Atelier Redon. He practised architecture in Moscow for five years, designing the city's Hotel Metropole (1898), and subsequently visiting Rome and London. Settling in London in 1907, he was first employed as a draughtsman to the architect Eustace Frere. He soon became a freelance draughtsman, producing presentation drawings for a number of leading architects to show their clients and to exhibit at the Royal Academy. His treatment of these drawings as works of art rather than technical exercises led to commissions from the Fine Art Society to visit Rome and Venice, and he held a total of eight solo shows with that dealer (1908-28). He also showed watercolours and etchings with leading exhibiting societies, and was elected to the membership of the Royal Society of Painter-Etchers and Engravers (ARE 1918, RE 1920) and the Royal Society of British Artists (1913). He was additionally a Fellow of the Royal Institute of British Architects (1922) and an associate of the British School in Rome. The most celebrated architectural draughtsman in England through the 1920s and 30s, he worked from studios in London, Oxford and Rome at the height of his career. However, when his practice collapsed, on the outbreak of the Second World War, he committed suicide at Hurstpierpoint, in Sussex, on 21 May 1943.

Further reading: *William Walcot*, London: Fine Art Society, 1974

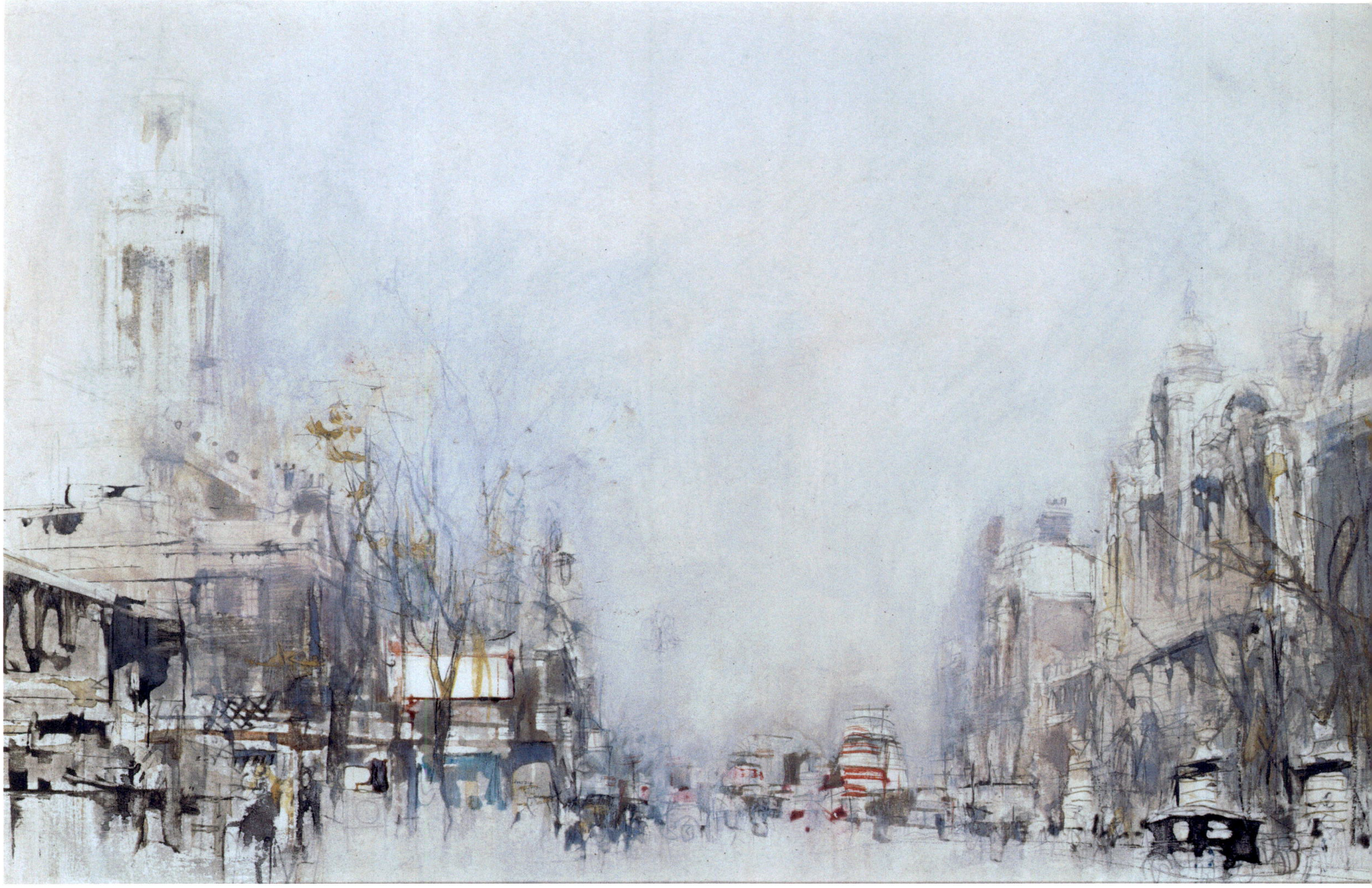

33. Marylebone Road *watercolour with ink and pencil, 5 ¾ x 8 ¾ inches*
Exhibited: Fine Art Society, September 1944

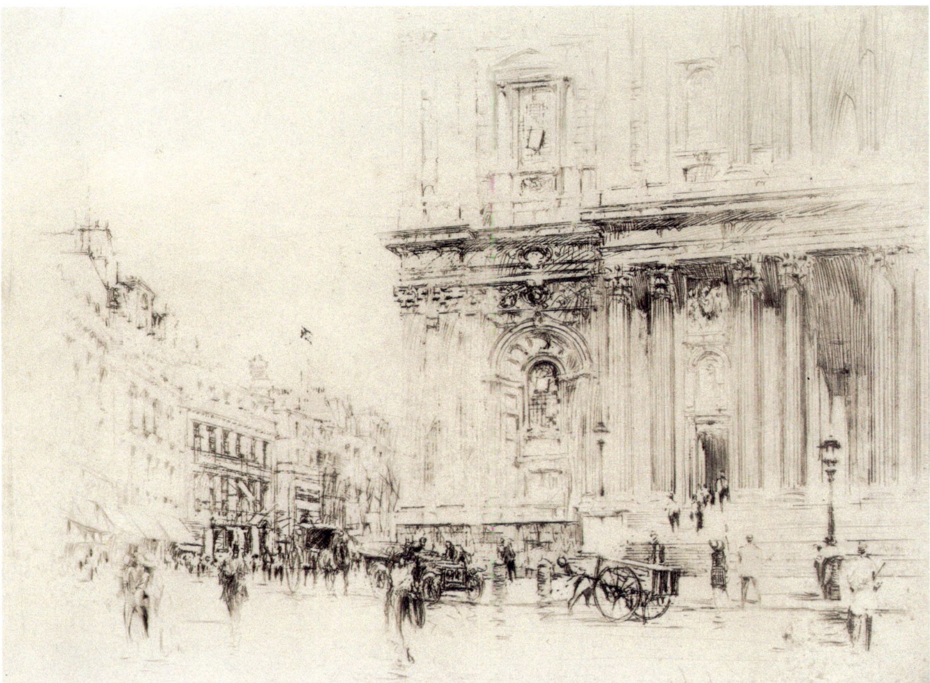

34. St Pauls
signed
etching with drypoint
7 ⅛ x 9 ¼ inches

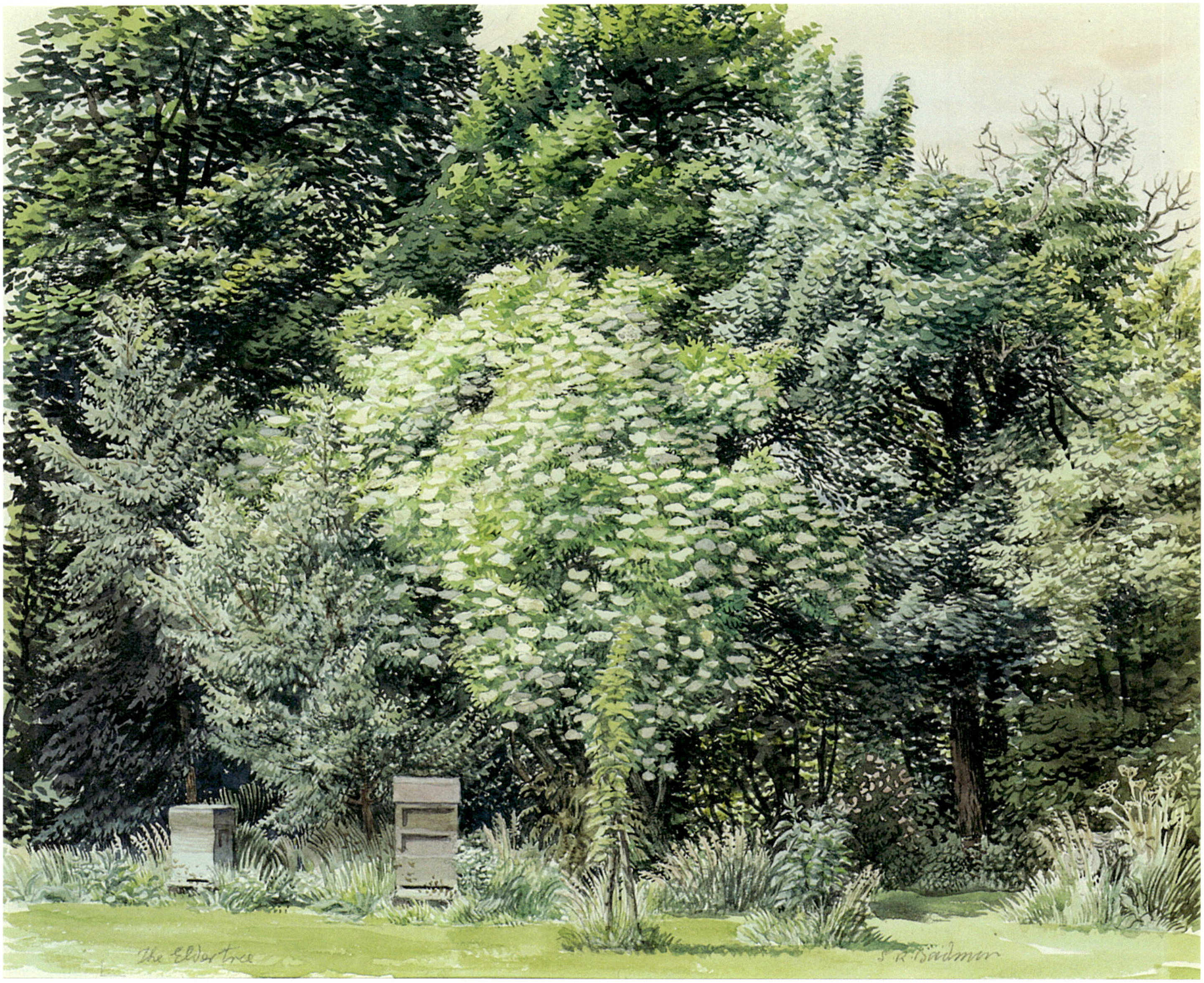

35. The Elder Tree *signed and inscribed with title, inscribed 'Leaf from a sketch book elder tree at Streamfield, Bigner 1969' below mount, signed with initials, inscribed with title and 'Drawn at Streamfield June 1969' on artist's label on original backboard, watercolour, 7 ¼ x 8 inches*
Exhibited: Royal Society of Painters in Water-Colours, Autumn 1969, no 26

Stanley Roy Badmin

Stanley Roy Badmin RE RWS AIA (1906-1989)

S R Badmin was born in Sydenham, London on 18 April 1906. He studied at Camberwell School of Art (1922-24) and the Royal College of Art (1924-27), and began his career by contributing illustrations to *The Graphic* (1927) and the *Tatler* (1928). In 1928, he qualified as a teacher, and supplemented his income by teaching at Richmond School of Art (1934) and St John's Wood School of Art (1936). However, he worked increasingly as an etcher and watercolourist, and was soon elected to the Royal Society of Painter-Etchers and Engravers (ARE 1931, RE 1935) and the Royal Society of Painters in Water-Colours (ARWS 1932, RWS 1939). He was also a member of the Artists' International Association. In 1933, he received a major commission – from the American magazine *Fortune* – to depict various towns in the United States; the results were exhibited in New York (1936). An important development in Badmin's illustrative style was marked soon after his return to England by *Highways and Byways of Essex* (1937), a collaboration with F L M Griggs. Even before the Second World War, he made a mark as an educational illustrator and was particularly admired for his accurate depiction of trees. Before working in the war, for the Ministry of Information and the Royal Air Force, he made a major contribution, in 1940, to Recording Britain – a term which might well be applied to his work as a whole.

From 1945, Badmin worked increasingly as a commercial artist, designing advertisements and posters, and producing illustrations for greetings cards and calendars. Equally in demand as an illustrator of books and periodicals, he published *Trees for Town and Country* (1947) and

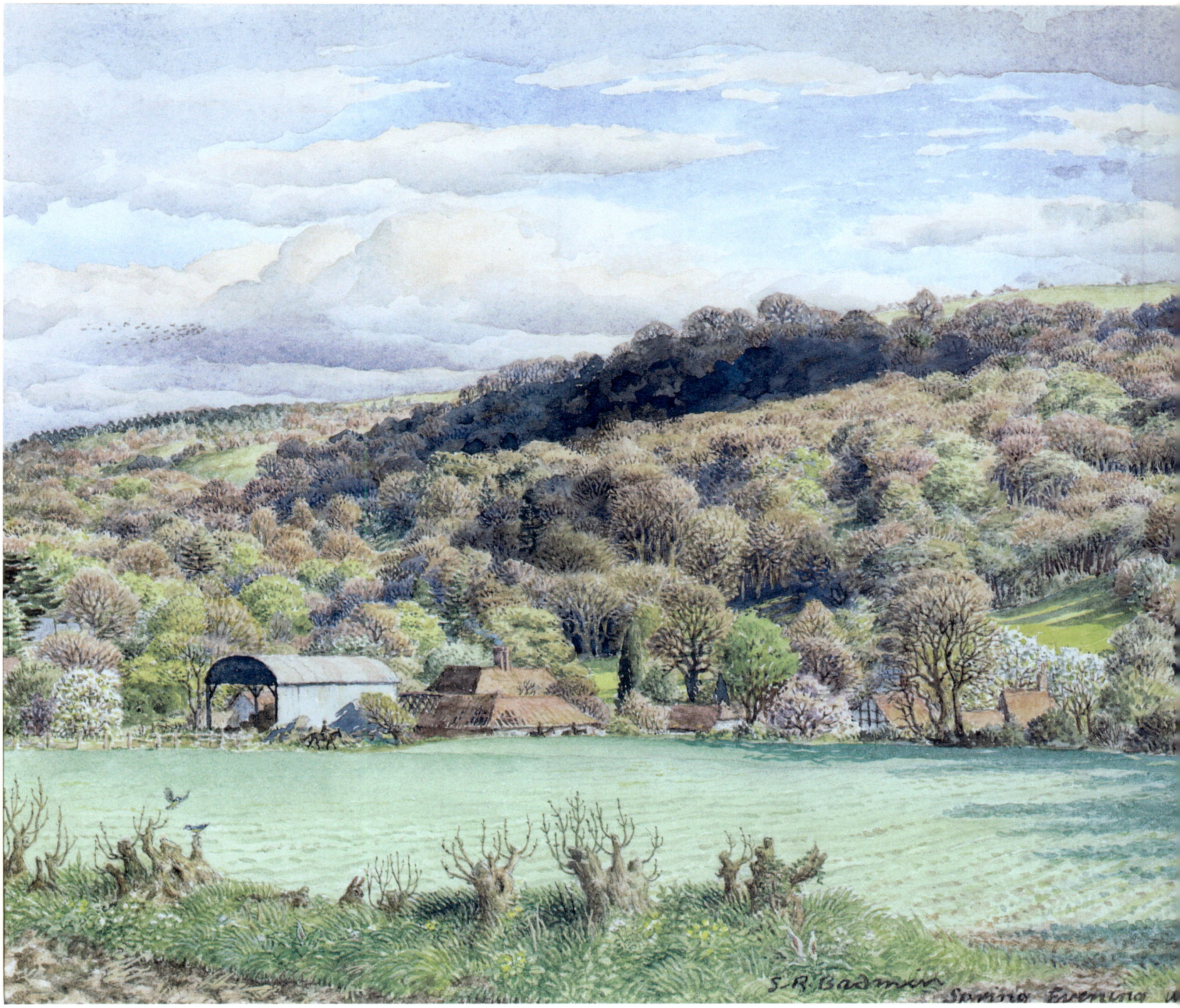

36. Spring Evening, West Burton, Sussex *signed and inscribed 'Spring Evening, W Burton, Sx,' signed and inscribed 'Spring Afternoon, W Burton' on artist's label on original backboard, watercolour, 7 x 9 ½ inches*
Exhibited: Royal Watercolour Society

contributed to the *Radio Times*. Only from the mid 1950s was he able to paint two or three major pieces for each RWS exhibition, and hold a show at the Leicester Galleries (1955). Even then, he found time to embark on projects for Shell: Geoffrey Grigson's *The Shell Guide to Trees and Shrubs* (1958) and four volumes of the series of 'Shell Guides to the Counties'. In 1959, he and his family moved to Bignor, near Pulborough, West Sussex, from where he continued to paint and exhibit. He held a further solo show, at the Worthing Art Gallery in 1967. In 1984, his achievement was honoured by the RWS in devoting a part of its Autumn Exhibition to his work.

Chris Beetles has played a major part in alerting the public to the importance of this ever pleasurable, quintessentially popular artist. He has published a monograph, with a catalogue raisonné of etchings, entitled *S R Badmin and The English Landscape* (Collins 1984) and mounted a major retrospective exhibition (1985).

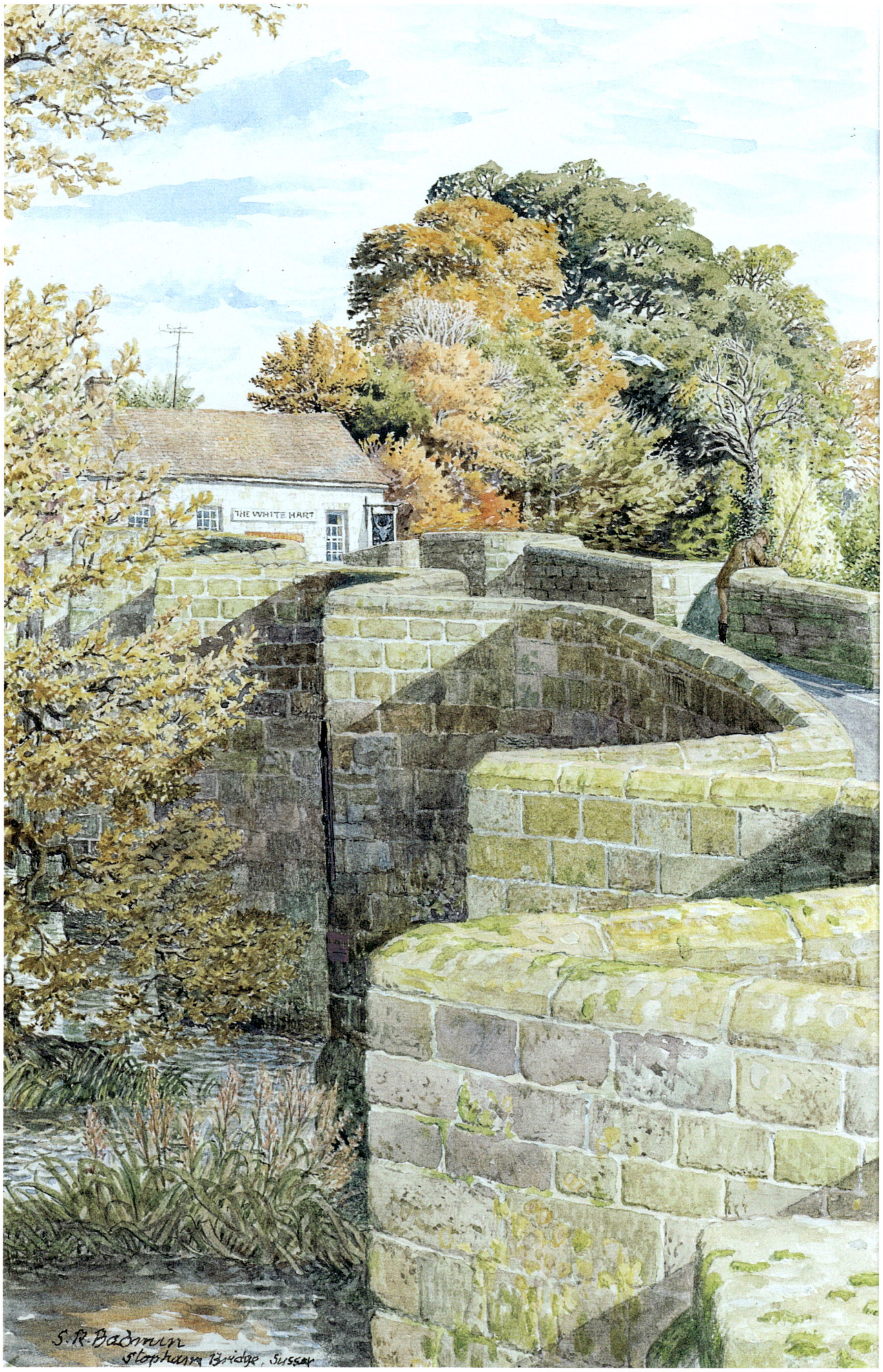

37. Stopham Bridge, Sussex *signed and inscribed with title, inscribed 'Stopham Bridge from W. Autumn. S R Badmin RWS. £350 March 1980' on reverse, signed and inscribed 'Stopham Bridge from NW' on artist's label on original backboard, watercolour and bodycolour, 8 x 5 inches*

Literature: Chris Beetles, *S R Badmin and The English Landscape*, London: Collins, 1985, pages 136-137

Exhibited: Petworth Festival of Music and Art, 1980

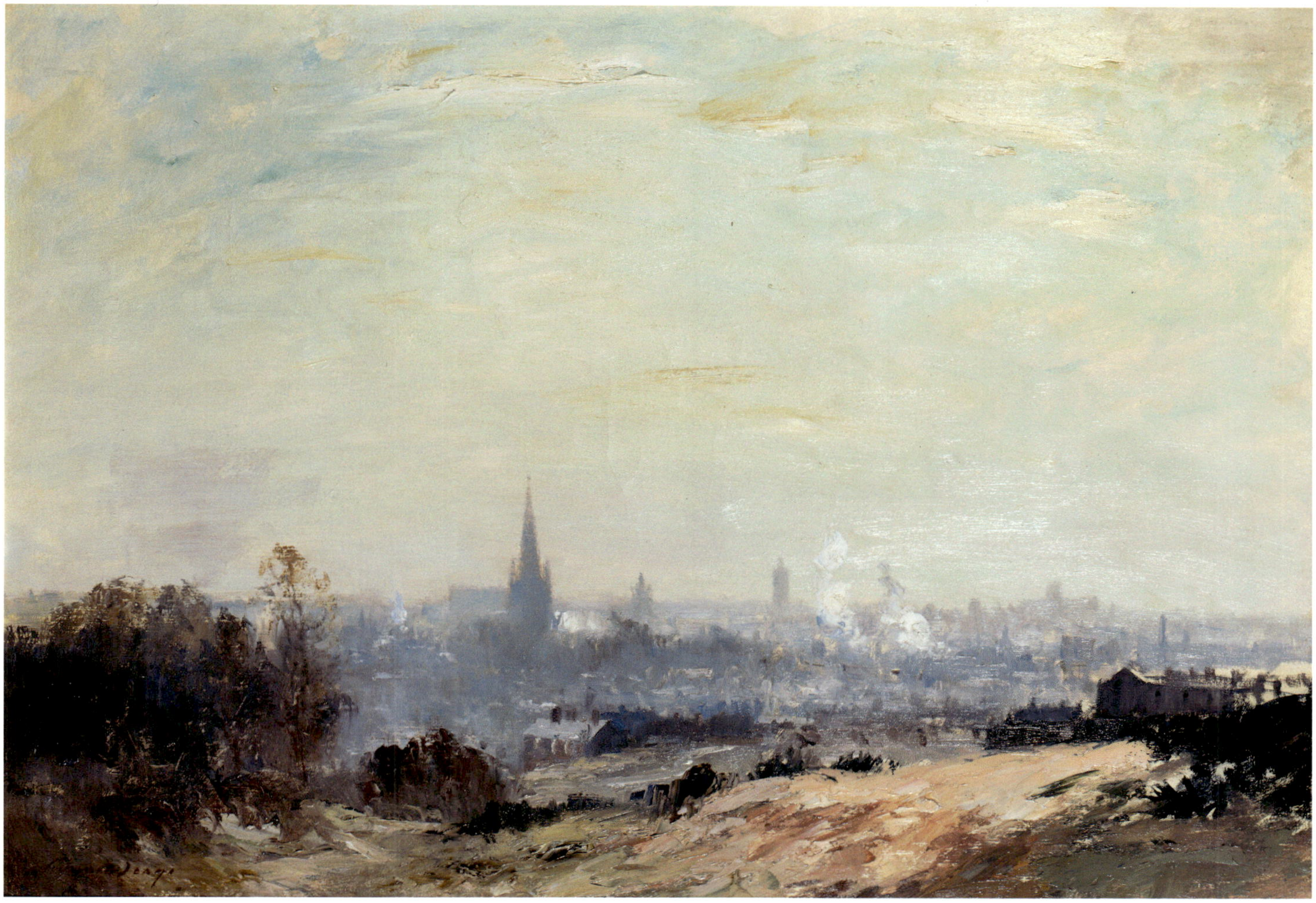

38. Autumn Morning – Norwich *signed, oil on canvas, 26 x 36 inches*
Literature: Francis W Hawcroft, *Edward Seago. A Review of the Years 1953-1964*, London: Collins, 1965, plate 2

Edward Seago

Edward Seago RBA RWS (1910-1974)

The son of a coal merchant, Edward Seago was born in Norwich, Norfolk on 31 January 1910. He was educated at South Lodge Preparatory School in Lowestoft and at Norwich Grammar School, but childhood illness meant that his schooling was frequently broken. As a result, he spent much time painting scenes from his bedroom window. Though given little encouragement by his parents, he received advice on art from Alfred Munnings and some instruction from Bernard Priestman. At the age of fourteen, he won a special prize from the Royal Drawing Society. About the age of eighteen, Seago joined Bevin's Travelling Show, and subsequently spent much time touring with circuses across Europe. He recorded these experiences in books and included a number of the illustrations in his first London solo show at the Sporting Gallery. In 1936, some forty-two of his paintings were used to accompany John Masefield's poems in *The Country Scene*, and he later worked with Masefield on *Tribute to the Ballet* (1937) and *A Generation Risen* (1942).

During the Second World War, Seago served with the Royal Engineers (1939-44) and spent much of his time in Italy painting with Field-Marshal Lord Alexander. An exhibition of his war paintings at Colnaghi's, in 1946, instigated a series of solo shows with that dealer. He enjoyed unprecedented success, with queues forming outside the gallery long before the doors opened: every exhibition sold out within an hour of opening. In addition, he submitted work regularly to exhibiting societies and was elected to the membership of the Royal Society of British Artists (1946) and the Royal Society of Painters in Water-Colours (ARWS 1957, RWS 1959). His autobiography, *A Canvas to Cover*, was published in 1947. In 1953, Seago was appointed one of the Official Artists of the Coronation, and three years later was invited by the Duke of Edinburgh to join the Royal Yacht, Britannia, on a round-the-world tour. The results of that trip were displayed at St James's Palace in 1957. While a keen traveller and sailor, he remained attached to East Anglia and lived at Ludham in Norfolk for many years. Following his death in London of a brain tumour on 19 January 1974, a memorial show was held at Marlborough Fine Art.

Further reading: James W Reid, *Edward Seago: The Landscape Art*, London: Sotheby's Publications, 1991

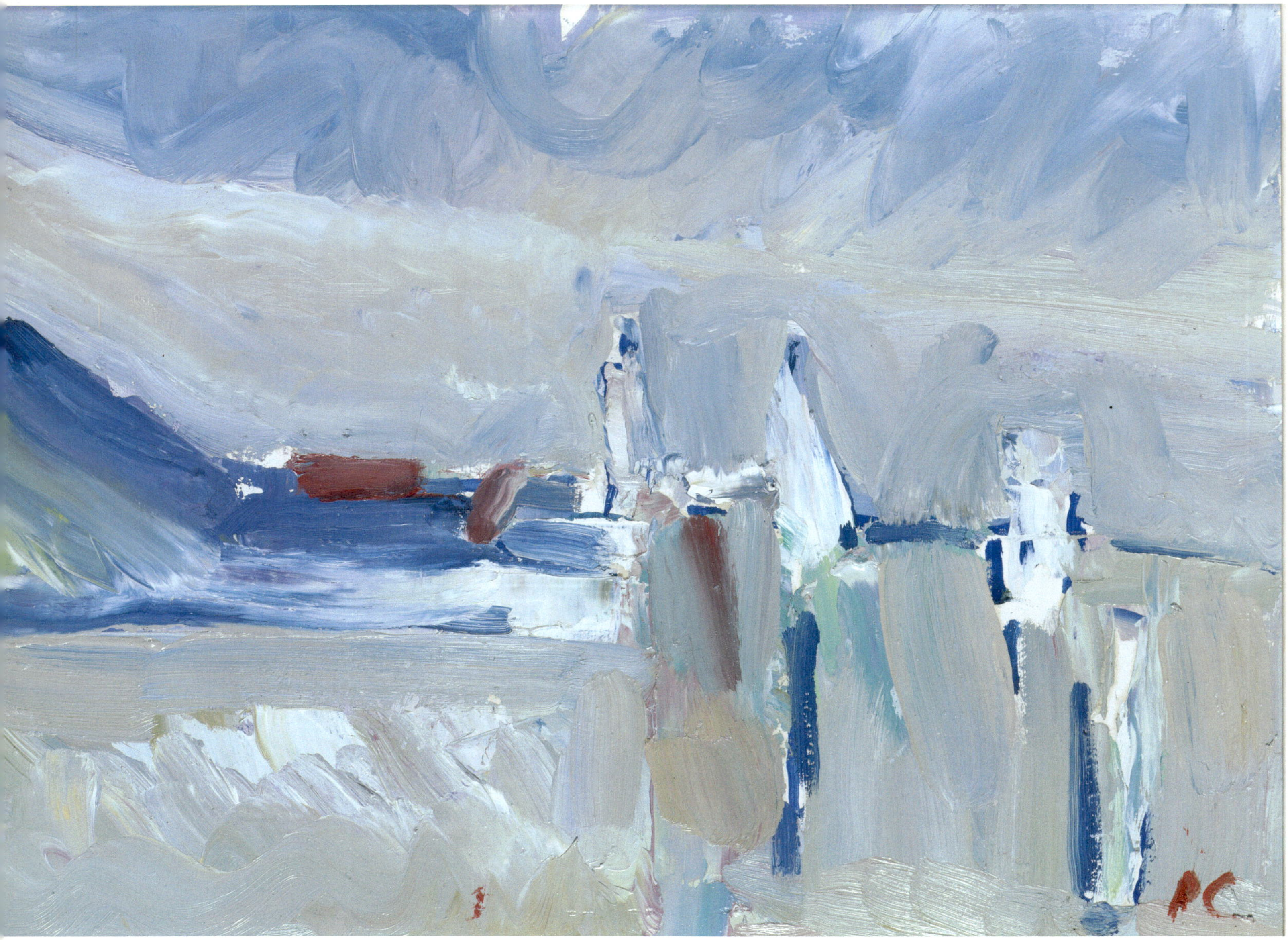

39. St-Valery-en-Caux *signed with initials, signed, inscribed with title and size and dated 2002 on reverse, oil on board, 12 x 16 inches*

Peter Coker

Peter Godfrey Coker RA (born 1926)

Peter Coker was born in London on 27 July 1926. He first studied at St Martin's School of Art (1941-43, 1947-50), and began to exhibit regularly at the Royal Academy from 1950. Though he was a contemporary of John Bratby and Edward Middleditch at the Royal College of Art (1950-54), his work related only briefly to the raw figuration of the Kitchen Sink School. This was signalled by his paintings of a Leytonstone butcher's shop which were included in his highly successful first solo show (Zwemmer Gallery, 1956). His development as a landscape painter originated in his first encounter with the canvases of Gustave Courbet on a trip to Paris (1950). By the mid 1950s, he was an established landscapist in the French manner, working from the motif on the coasts of Normandy (1955) and Brittany (1957), and drawing inspiration from such contemporaries as Nicolas de Stäel. Later in the decade, he revived the spirit of Barbizon in his paintings of Epping Forest (as is exemplified by *Forest VI*, included here).

Coker moved with his family to Manningtree in Essex (1962), and added occasional appearances at Colchester School of Art to teaching at St Martin's. Nevertheless, he concentrated on his work, and made time for painting trips to France, the North of England and Scotland. He held solo shows at the Zwemmer Gallery (1960s), the Thackeray Gallery (1970s) and Gallery 10 (1980s), and continued to exhibit regularly at the Royal Academy. He was elected an Academician (ARA 1965, RA 1972), and had his early images of the butcher's shop presented at the RA in one of an increasing number of public retrospectives (1979).

From 1972, Coker made several visits to Bargemon, Provence, during which he gradually accepted the character of the South of France, and

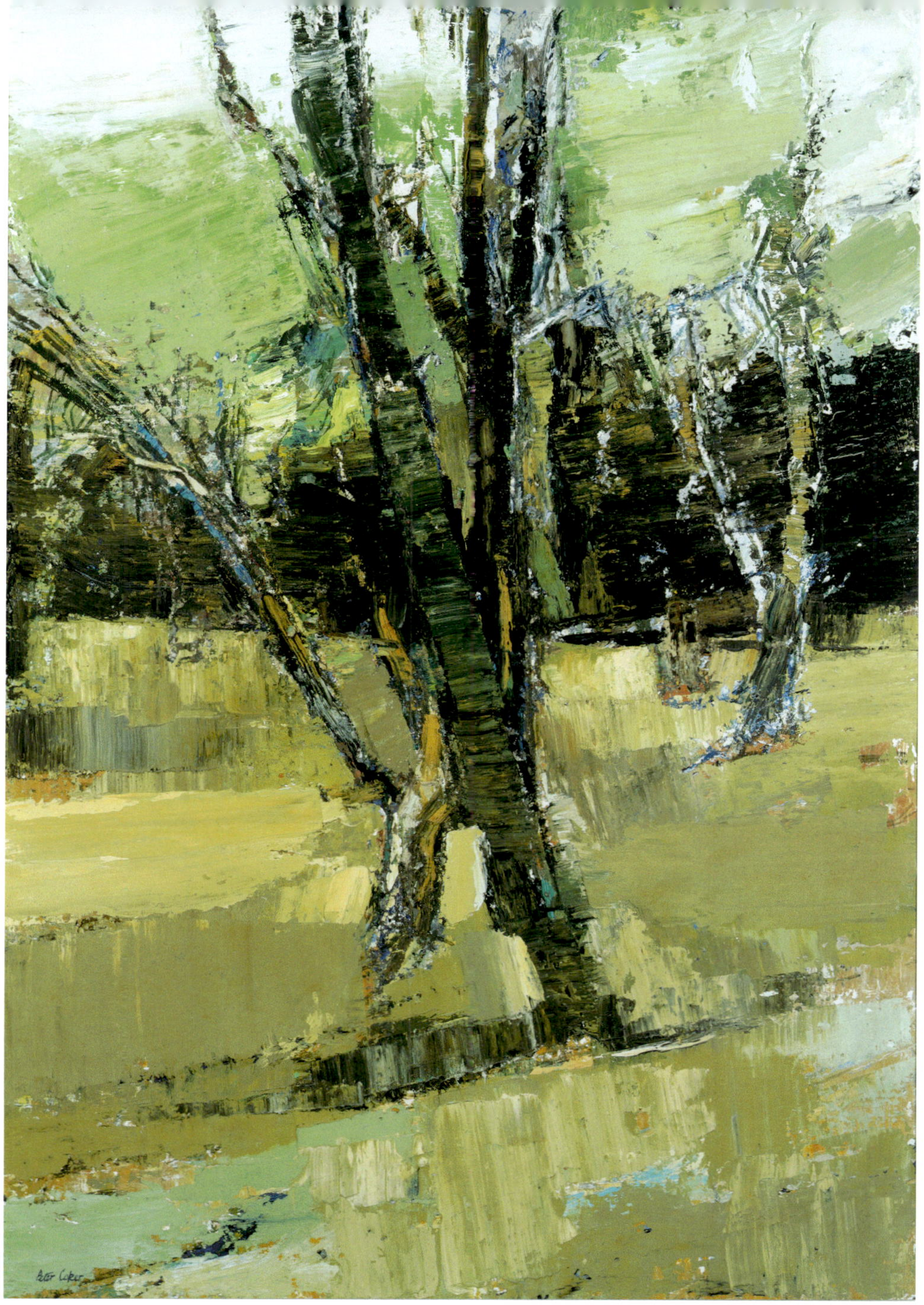

40. Forest VI *oil on board, 58 ½ x 40 inches*
Exhibited: *Peter Coker*, Zwemmer Gallery, 1959, no 11; *Peter Coker*, The Minories, Colchester and touring, 1972-73, no 21; *British Painting 1952-1977*, Royal Academy of Arts, 1977, no 223; *Peter Coker*, Abbot Hall Art Gallery, Kendal and touring, 1992-93, no 4
Literature: David Wootton, *Peter Coker RA*, London: Chris Beetles Ltd, 2002, page 65 and catalogue raisonné no 77

integrated its startling light and colour into his established palette and handling. Late in the decade, he applied this approach to an ideal motif, in beginning a series of paintings of the garden of the Clos du Peyronnet, Menton. Following the death of his son Nicholas in 1985, he stayed at Badenscallie, Ross-shire, Scotland. There he began an impassioned series of landscapes, extended on subsequent visits, which focussed on salmon nets drying at Achiltibuie. These reaffirmed his essential identity as 'a northern painter', which had actually become more strongly emphasised by his contrasting achievement of painting the south. The many studies and paintings inspired by both Mediterranean France and the West of Scotland comprised important elements of such recent retrospectives as that of drawings and sketchbooks at the Fitzwilliam Museum (1989) and that of paintings and drawings at Abbot Hall Art Gallery (1992).

In October 2002, Chris Beetles mounted a major retrospective of the work of Peter Coker and, at the same time, launched the artist's authorised biography. The beautifully produced hardback book, with over 250 illustrations, contains contributions from Richard Humphreys (Tate Gallery), John Russell Taylor (*The Times*), and David Wootton (Chris Beetles Ltd). The book includes a comprehensive biography and chronology, essays, appraisals of his work, a catalogue raisonné and lists of his exhibitions and sketchbooks.

While the monograph and retrospective were being planned, it seemed that the artist's career might have been drawing to a close. However, the joint project revived his energies significantly. This has been manifested by a range of new work shown at Chris Beetles Ltd during Spring 2004. The motifs are mostly familiar, being drawn from existing sketchbooks, and range across France and encompass Britain. Yet the handling is freer than ever, and the palette more vibrant – accomplishments of which Peter is justifiably proud. This display has been complemented by an exhibition of recent Parisian subjects, touring to Gainsborough's House, Sudbury, the Royal Academy of Arts, and Graves Art Gallery, Sheffield.

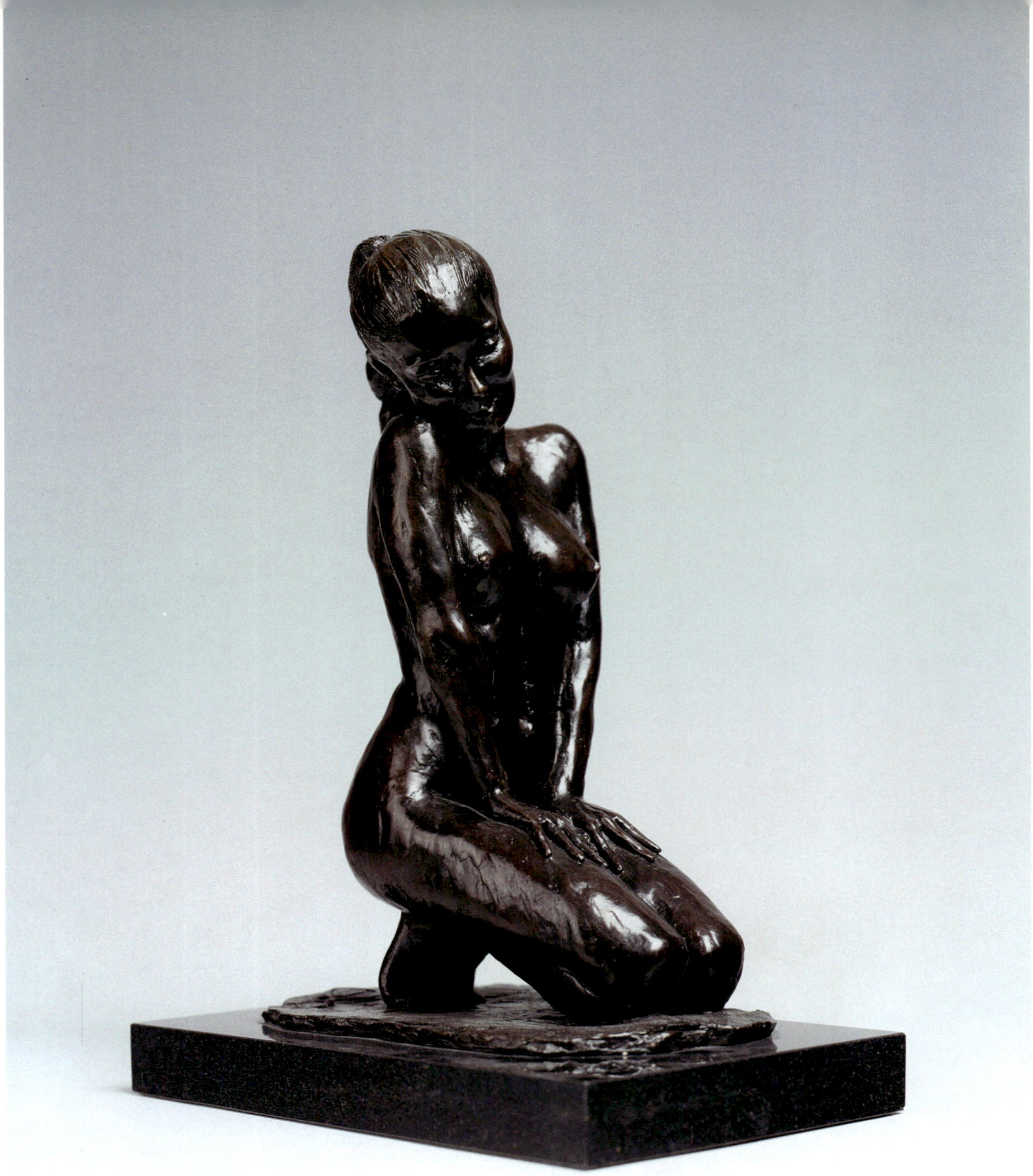

◀ **41. Joni crouching**
stamped with the foundry and sculptor's mark and numbered 10/12, 12 ½ inches high, number 10 from an edition of 12
Literature: Carol Plazzotta and Richard O'Conor, *Enzo Plazzotta. A Catalogue Raisonné*, London: Trefoil Books, 1986, no 316
Exhibited: Bedford College, London, July-August 1980; Richmond Gallery, October 1980; Bruton Gallery, Bruton, Somerset, November 1980- January 1981

42. Christ and Mary: Maquette ▶
signed with monogram and numbered 2/12, bronze, 12 inches high including base, number 2 from an edition of 12
Literature: T S R Boase (critical essay), *The Sculpture of David Wynne 1949-1967*, London: Michael Joseph, 1968, page 100
Exhibited: *An Exhibition of New Sculpture by David Wynne*, Arthur Tooth & Sons, May-June 1964, no 17
This is the maquette for *Christ and Mary Magdalene*, 1963, which stands at the Chaplain's Quadrangle, Magdalen College, Oxford, and the south transcept of Ely Cathedral.

Enzo Plazzotta
Enzo Plazzotta (1921-1981)

Enzo Plazzotta was born in Mestre, near Venice on 29 May 1921, and grew up on the shores of Lake Maggiore. Developing a particular aptitude for sculpture, he began to study under Messina at the Accademia di Brera, in Milan, at the age of seventeen. However, he had to terminate his studies abruptly when Italy entered the Second World War. A volunteer in the Bersaglieri, he was sent to North Africa, where he was awarded the Silver Medal for valour. Following the fall of Mussolini in 1943, he broke with the Fascist regiment and helped to found a partisan group in the Italian mountains. Betrayed by an infiltrator, he was captured and placed in solitary confinement, escaping six months later while in transit to Mauthausen. In Switzerland, he helped to improve relations between the partisans and the Allies. In the closing months of the war, he returned to Italy to participate in the final struggle for national liberation.

Plazzotta was finally able to return to the Brera to complete his studies, under Manzù, who exerted a considerable influence over his work. On graduating, he received a commission from the Italian Committee of Liberation to make a bronze statuette for presentation to the British Special Forces Club. He travelled to London himself to present the statuette and was so drawn to the British way of life that he decided to stay.

Plazzotta found work as a portrait artist but later, with a family to support, he was obliged to turn to more lucrative pursuits. Rather than practise his art merely as a hobby, he set up a commercial art agency in London, which specialised in importing Milanese art and design. It was not until the early 1960s that he found himself in a position to take up sculpting again. Engaging himself fully in his work, he produced both accessible pieces and more personal projects in which he overcame conceptual and technical problems. Favourite preoccupations included dancing figures, horses and adaptations of classical and Christian themes. Retaining close links with his native Italy, he kept a small studio in Pietrasanta, near Carrara; it was the base for much casting of his work, and for experiments in carving marble and onyx. In 1976 he received the title of Cavaliere from the Italian government for services to art. In the same year he moved into the Garden Studio in Cathcart Road, built and formerly owned by the sculptor, Sir Charles Wheeler. He contracted cancer in 1981 and died in the same year.

David Wynne

David Wynne OBE (born 1926)

David Wynne was born in Lyndhurst, Hampshire on 25 May 1926, and was educated at private preparatory schools and at Stowe. Going up to Cambridge to read Zoology at Trinity College, he had to interrupt his studies in 1944, to serve in the Royal Navy during the Second World War. A posting to the Far East gave him an opportunity to engage with striking examples of ancient religious sculpture, and so begin to appreciate sculpture as a timeless means of communication. On returning to Cambridge, in 1947, he was given special dispensation to study Art History, under Professor Andrew Gow, and develop his sculptural skills. By the time he left university, two years later, he had decided to become a sculptor.

At the outset of his career, Wynne received encouragement from a number of significant sculptors, including Jacob Epstein, Georg Erlich and Paul Landowski. As a result, he was able to dispense with more formal training, and soon developed into an assured figurative artist with a willingness to experiment with both material and subject matter. Preoccupations with portraiture, religious themes and animal forms, and more generally the body in movement, established themselves during the first decade of his career. And, while most of his earliest pieces are in bronze, he soon made use of silver and aluminium, many kinds of stone, and even ivory.

Wynne first exhibited in *Artists of Fame and Promise* at the Leicester Galleries in 1950, and subsequently held solo shows both there (1955, 1959) and at Tooth's (1964, 1966). One of the most distinctive and popular works produced in this period was *Guy the Gorilla* (1961), in fossil marble, which arose from a commission from the London County Council.

Further shows took place in London, at the Temple Gallery (drawings, 1964) and the Covent Garden Gallery (1970, 1971) at the Fitzwilliam Museum, Cambridge (portrait heads, 1972); and in New York, at the Findlay Galleries (1967, 1969, 1973).

During the 1970s, Wynne gained a new popularity, designing the fifty pence coin with the motif of linked hands to commemorate the entry of Great Britain into the Common Market (1973) and also the Queen's Jubilee Medal (1977). He was the subject of two BBC television documentaries: *One Pair of Hands* (1977) and the series *Taking Shape* (1978). A retrospective exhibition at Cannizaro Park, Wimbledon (1980) helped to remind the public of his achievement to date.

Since then, Wynne's major commissions have included the Lion and Unicorn figures for the Queen Elizabeth Gate, in Hyde Park (1993), and two large-scale religious works: *The Risen Christ* and *Seraphim* in limestone for the West Front of Wells Cathedral (1985), and the *Virgin Mary* in polychromed portland stone for the Lady Chapel at Ely Cathedral (2000). This last is sited in the same building as a full-scale version of the work included here.

Further reading: T S R Boase (critical essay), *The Sculpture of David Wynne 1949-1967*, London: Michael Joseph, 1968; Graham Hughes (introduction), *The Sculpture of David Wynne 1968-1974*, London: Phaidon, 1974; Jonathan Stone (Editor), *The Sculpture of David Wynne 1974-1992*, London: Lund Humphries, 1993

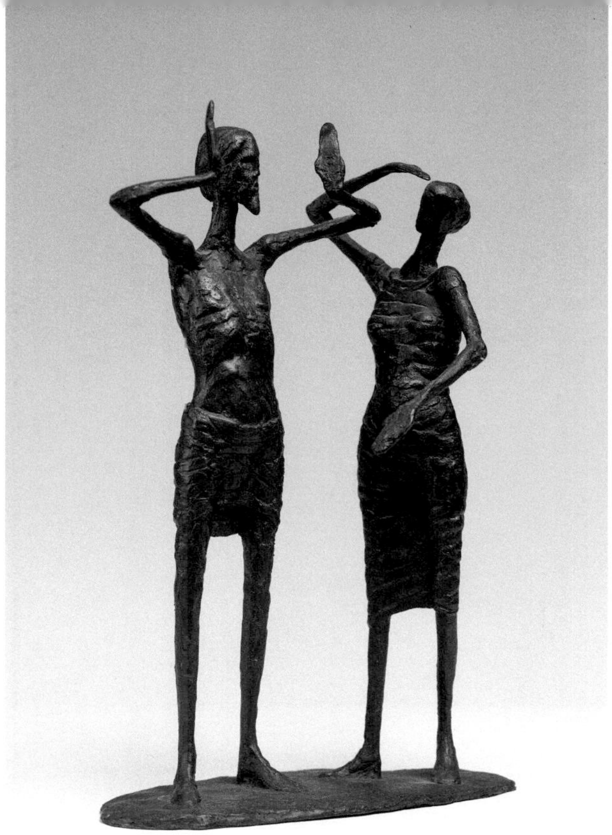

Christ and Mary: Maquette

> *Jesus saith unto her, 'Touch me not; for I am not yet ascended to my Father: but go to my brethren, and say to them, I ascend unto my Father, and your Father; and to my God, and your God.'*
> (*The Gospel According to St John*, Chapter 20)

In 1963, David Wynne began a series of studies from the nude model, focussing on the female form, which evolved into an exploration of the relationship between two figures. The theme culminated in the life-sized *Christ and Mary Magdalene*, representing the moving encounter between these protagonists on the first Easter Day. Its particular qualities – equally manifest in the present maquette – were sensitively described by T S R Boase in a study of Wynne's early sculpture:

> *In the central themes of the Christian religion there is a mingling of the spiritual and the corporeal, of inspiration and bodily shape, that has always found a response in the visual arts. This moment of insight in the garden has an intensity and compassion that speak across very differing concepts of style. Wynne's tall gaunt forms, the Magdalene vaguely contemporary in her dress, are very different from that sudden renewal of hope that Fra Angelico painted in the cell of San Marco, or the sensuously ecstatic 'Rabboni-Master' of the sweeping curves of Titian's reunion. The pattern of these thin arms and flattened hands are nearer to a more contemporary Italian master, Alberto Giacometti; but the passion in it is a very individual statement. Christ is a figure from the grave and a terrible death, austere but dazzling in its self revelation, and the movement of Mary's arm as she shields her eyes from the blinding force of His gaze has all Wynne's accuracy of observation. It was presented by a donor, in memory of his brother, to Magdalen College, Oxford.*
> (*The Sculpture of David Wynne 1949-1967*, London: Michael Joseph, 1968, page 14)

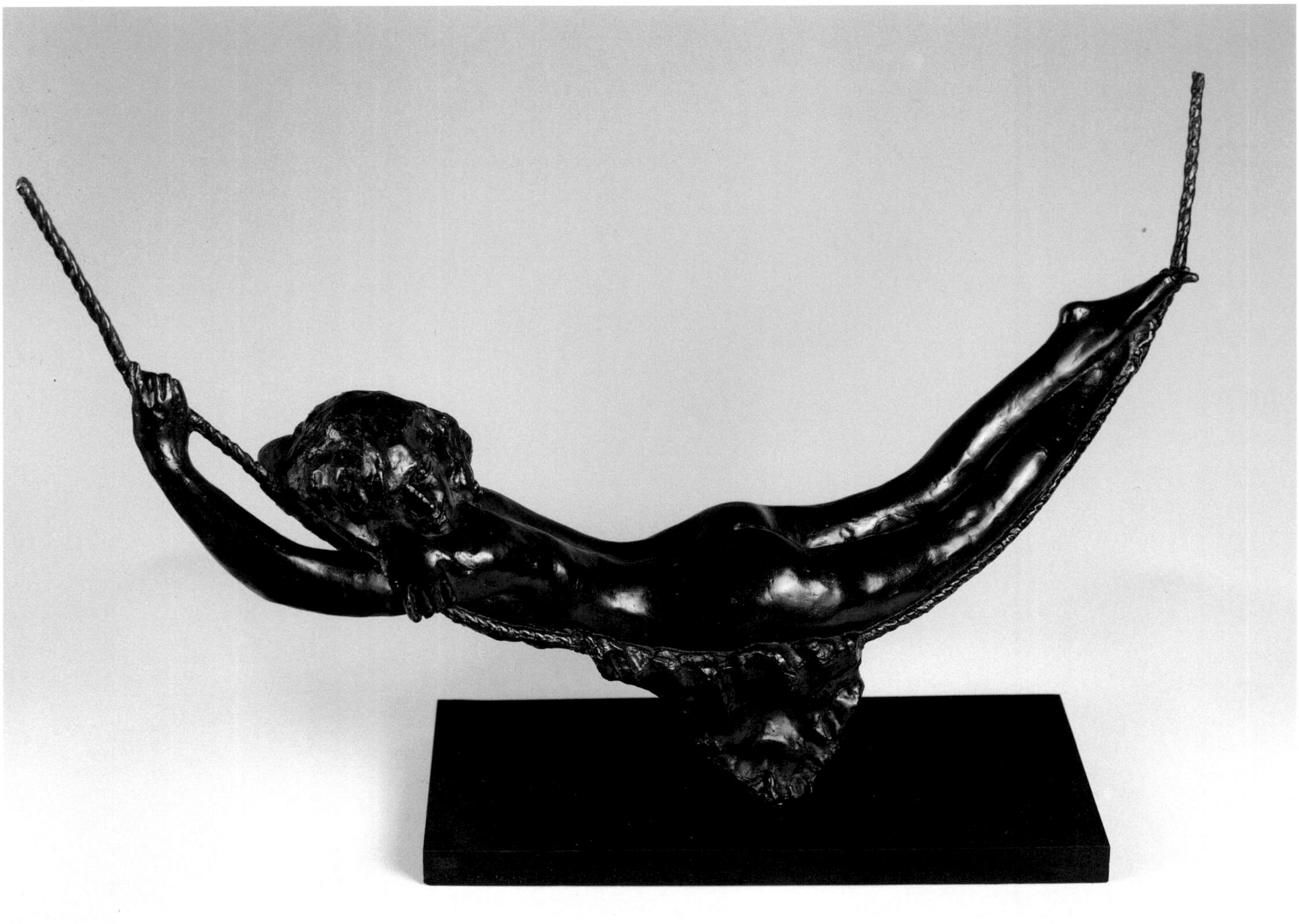

43. Nude on a Hammock *signed and numbered 5/9, bronze, 18 ½ inches high x 29 ½ inches long, no 5 from an edition of 9*
Exhibited: *Summer Exhibition*, Royal Academy of Arts, 1980, no 1183

Sydney Harpley

Sydney Charles Harpley RA FRBS (1927-1992)

Sydney Harpley was born in Fulham, London on 9 April 1927. The son of an electrician and cabinet maker, he grew up in Dagenham, and spent the war years as an evacuee in Berkshire and Bedfordshire. Though talented in both art and music, he left school at the age of fourteen to take up an apprenticeship as an electrician. He went on to work at an American air base, and would later cite aircraft as a formative influence on his artistic development, describing planes as 'sculptures in space'. Even more instrumental in his decision to become a sculptor was his encounter with the carved head of Ramases II, in Cairo, during National Service with the Royal Engineers (1945-48). On his return home, he took evening classes in drawing while working at a factory in Roehampton making artificial limbs. In 1951, he became a full-time student of sculpture at Hammersmith School of Art, and two years later began to study under John Skeaping at the Royal College of Art.

While still a student, Harpley established the single female figure as his favourite form; he exhibited examples at the Young Contemporaries and at the Royal Academy, and sold his first pieces to the National Gallery of New Zealand and the artist Fleur Cowles. In 1956, the year of his first marriage, he returned to Hammersmith as a part-time teacher and began to receive commissions for portrait busts and public figure groups. In 1963, he fully established himself, winning a competition to create a portrait memorial to Jan Smuts, and being elected to the fellowship of the Royal Society of British Sculptors. From 1972, he taught part-time at Leicester Polytechnic, and while there met his second wife Jo, an art historian specialising in costume. Marrying in 1981, they moved to Radigan Farm, Somerset (1986) and then to Kilkenny, in Ireland (1989). At the height of his career, Harpley became a Royal Academician (ARA 1974, RA 1981) and had a number of successful international solo shows, including two at the Chris Beetles Gallery in 1987 and 1990. He died in Dublin on 9 March 1992.

The Estate of Sydney Harpley is represented by Chris Beetles Limited.

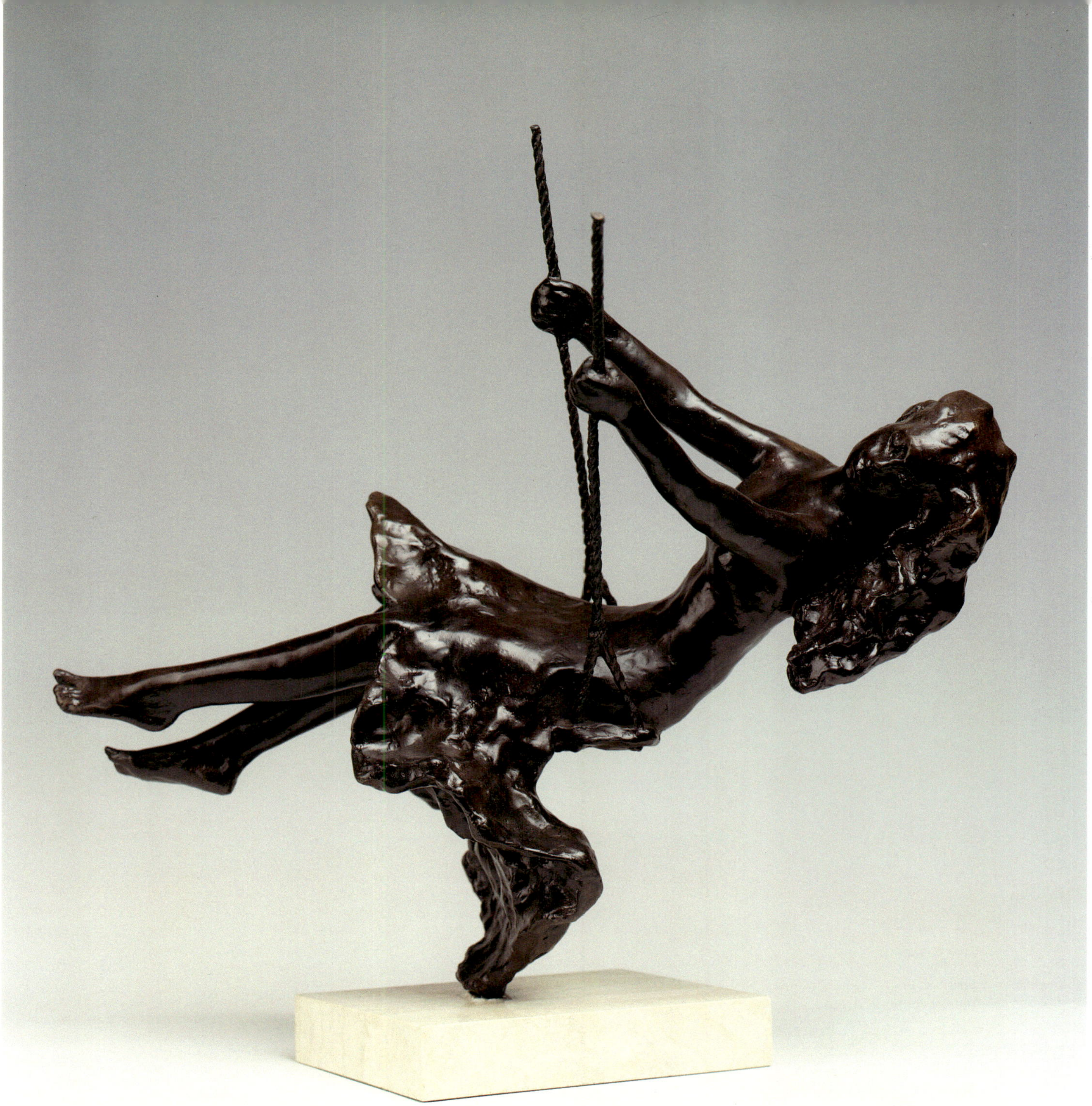

44. Girl on a Swing *signed, bronze, the artist's proof of an edition of eight, 21 ½ inches high x 22 inches long*

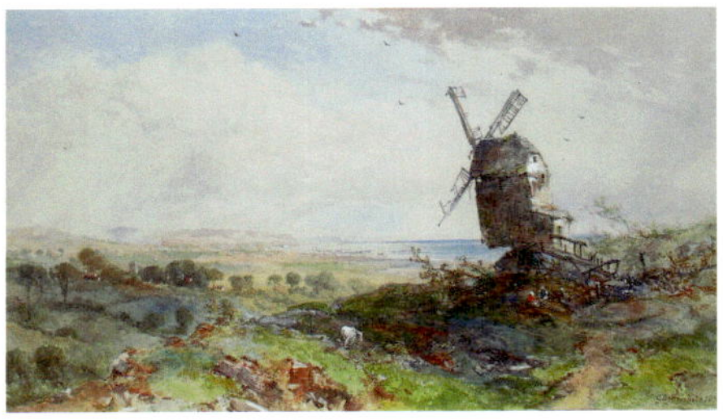

45

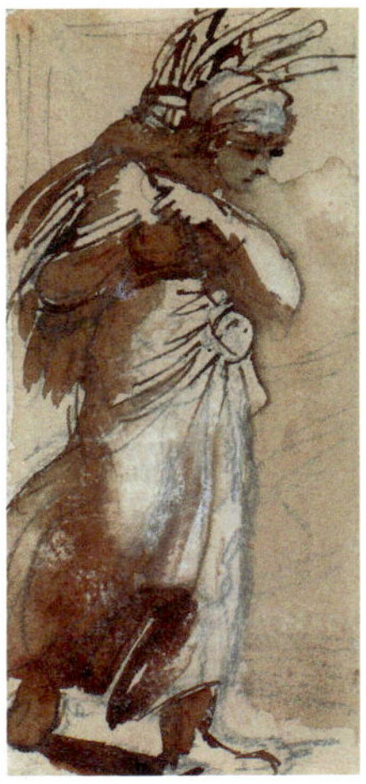

46

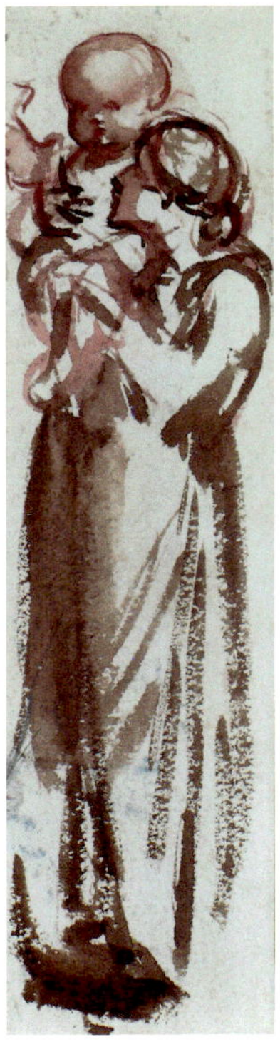

47

Charles Branwhite
Charles Branwhite, AOWS (1817-1880)

Charles Branwhite was born in Bristol, and studied in the city under his father, Nathan Cooper Branwhite, and William Muller. He then specialised in landscapes of the West Country in oil and watercolour, which he exhibited in London.

45. Between Clevedon and Weston
signed and dated 1875, watercolour, 16 ½ x 28 ½ inches

Louisa, Marchioness of Waterford
Louisa Anne de la Poer Beresford, Marchioness of Waterford (née Stuart) (1818-1891)

For a biography of the Marchioness of Waterford, please refer to *Chris Beetles Summer Show*, 2001, page 21.

46. Gathering Wood
monochrome watercolour, 6 x 2 ¾ inches

47. Madonna and Child
monochrome watercolour, 8 x 2 ¼ inches

48. Conversation
watercolour, 6 ¼ x 4 ¾ inches

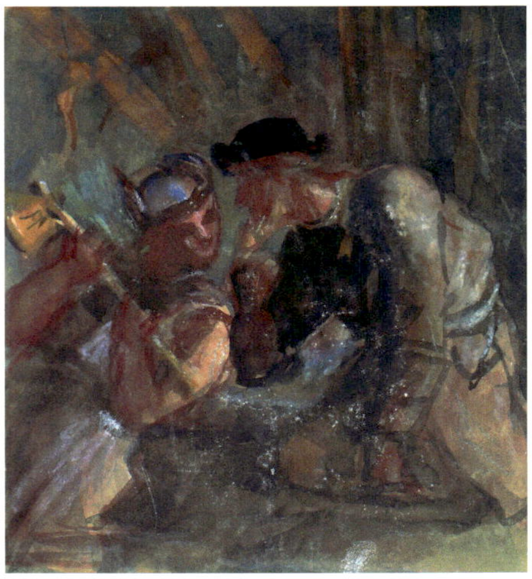

48

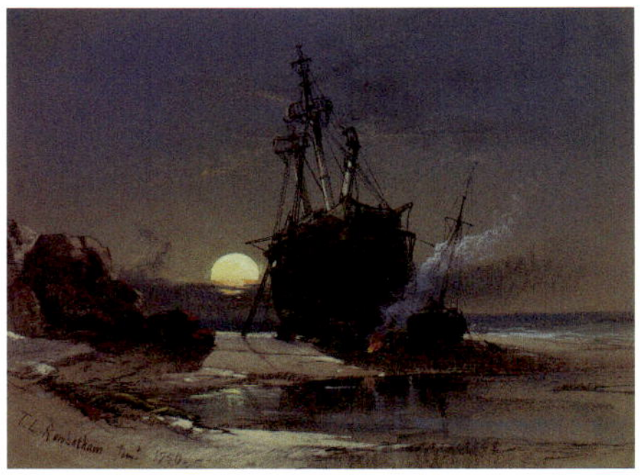

49

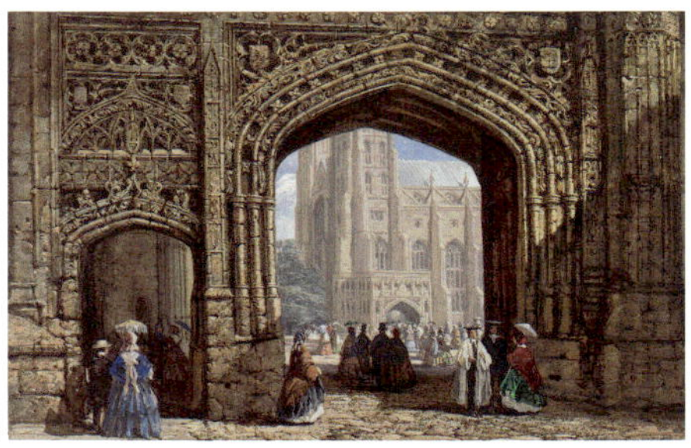

50

Thomas Leeson Rowbotham
Thomas Charles Leeson Rowbotham, NWS (1823-1875)

Thomas Leeson Rowbotham was born in Dublin. He took lessons from his father, a landscape and marine painter, and later succeeded him as drawing master at the Royal Naval School, Greenwich. He specialised in romantic landscape watercolours, including views of the Italian Lakes, which he never visited, producing a number of chromolithographs.

49. Moonlight
signed and dated June 1850, coloured chalk, charcoal with bodycolour on tinted paper, 8 x 10 ½ inches

Louise Rayner
Louise Rayner (1832-1924)

For a biography of Louise Rayner, please refer to *Chris Beetles Summer Show*, 1998, page 26.

50. Canterbury Cathedral
signed, watercolour and bodycolour, 11 x 16 ½ inches

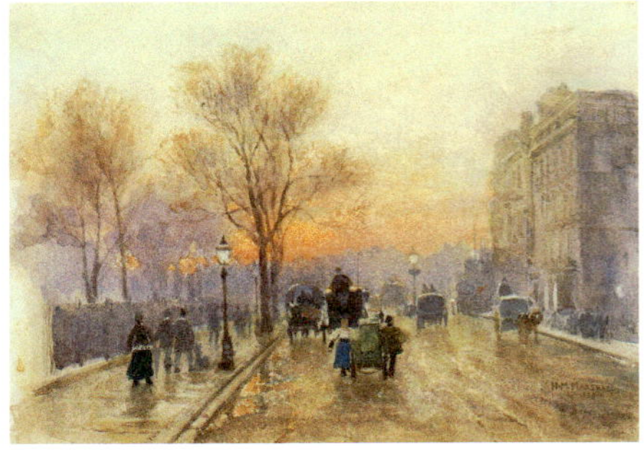

51

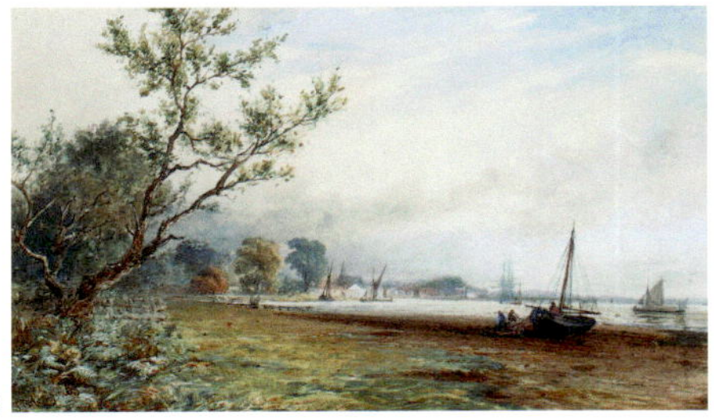

52

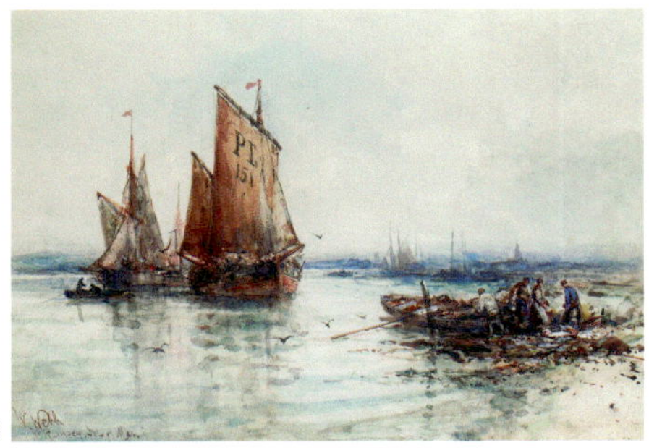

53

Herbert Menzies Marshall
Herbert Menzies Marshall, RWS (1841-1913)

For a biography of the Herbert Menzies Marshall, please refer to *Chris Beetles Summer Show*, 1998, page 68.

51. Sunset, Piccadilly
signed and dated 1888, watercolour, 6 x 8 inches

Thomas Bush Hardy
Thomas Bush Hardy, RBA (1842-1897)

Sheffield-born Thomas Bush Hardy became greatly popular as a marine painter. His best work was often on a small scale, and depicted Venice and the coasts of Norfolk and the Netherlands. His son was the illustrator and poster designer, Dudley Hardy.

52. The Estuary, Low Tide
signed & dated 65, watercolour with bodycolour, 8 ¼ x 13 ¾ inches

William Edward Webb
William Edward Webb (1862-1903)

William Edward Webb lived in Manchester and specialised in native marine subjects.

53. Near Ramsey, Isle of Man
signed and inscribed with title, watercolour heightened with bodycolour, 9 ½ x 13 ½ inches

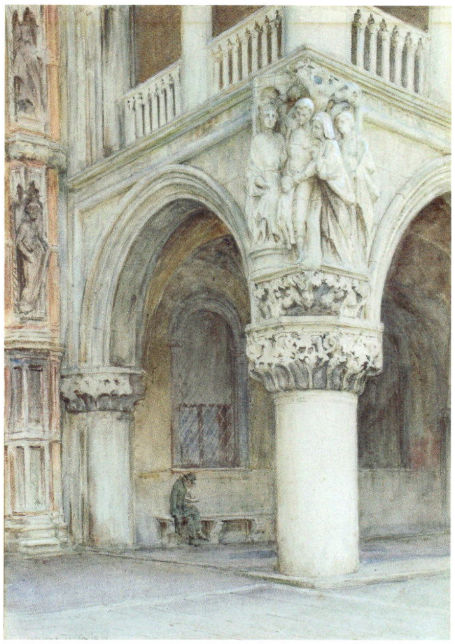

54

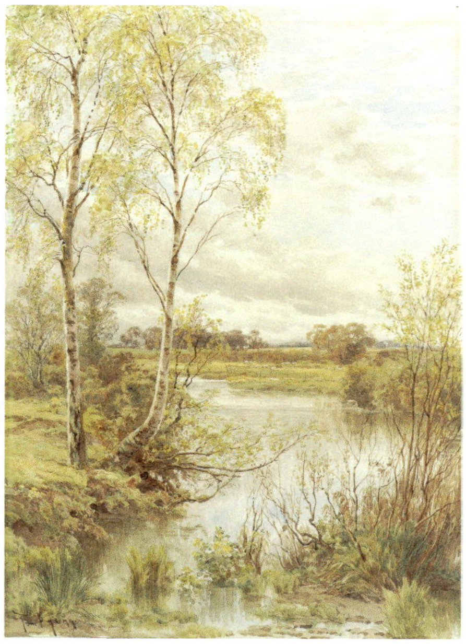

56

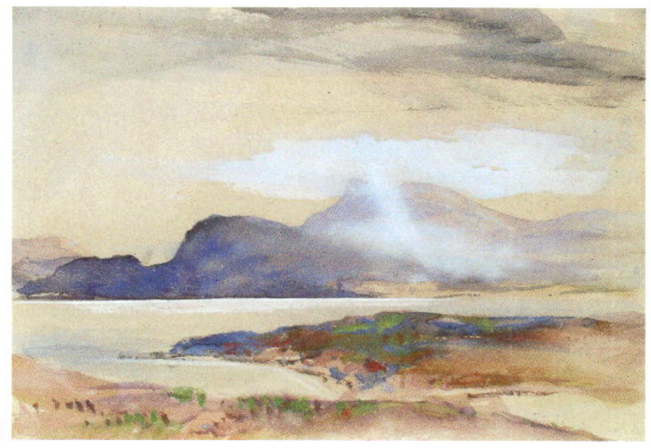

58

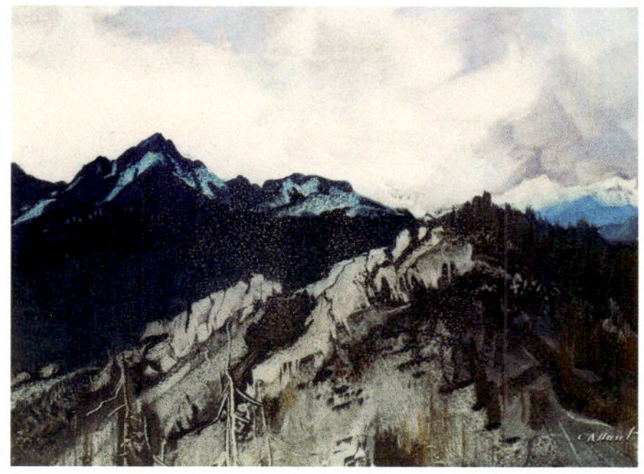

59

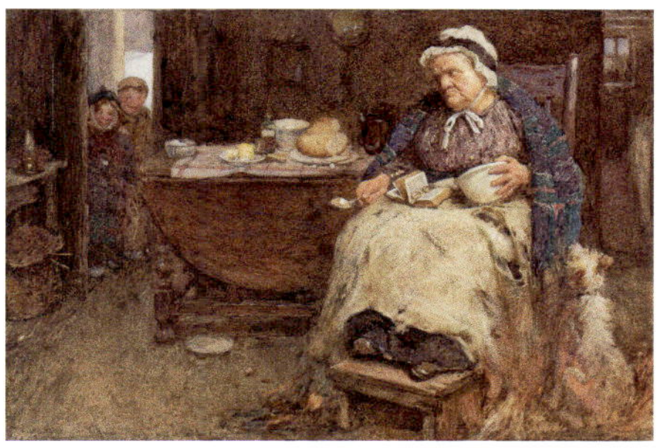

55

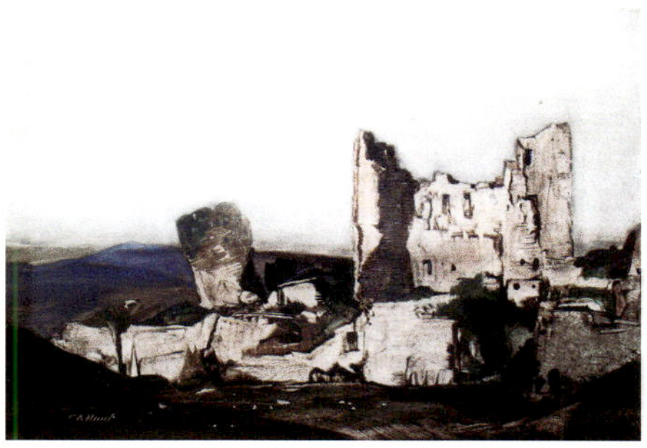

57

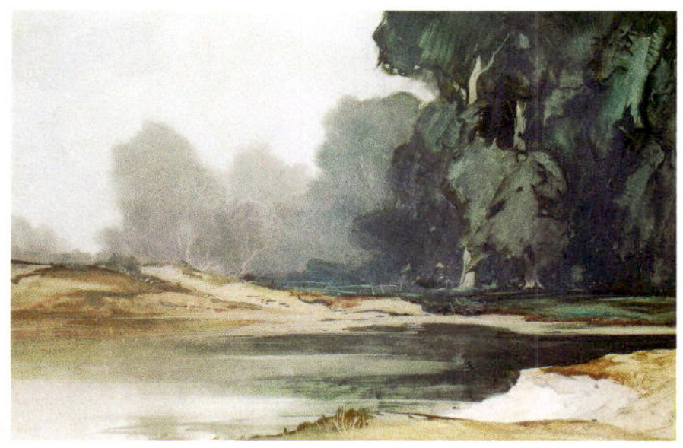

60

Walter Tyndale

Walter Tyndale, RI (1855-1943)

For a biography of Walter Tyndale, please refer to *Chris Beetles Summer Show*, 2003, page 16.

54. Doge's Palace, Venice

signed, watercolour, 9 ¾ x 14 inches

John Henry Henshall

John Henry Henshall, RWS (1856-1928)

Lancashire-born John Henry Henshall studied in London, at the South Kensington Schools and the Royal Academy Schools. Becoming a figure and portrait painter in oil and watercolour, he often produced large-scale genre and historical scenes. Exhibiting widely, he was a member of the Manchester Academy of Fine Arts as well as the Royal Society of Painters in Water-Colours.

55. Joining Grandma for Tea

signed, watercolour, 7 ¾ x 11 ¾ inches

Thomas Hunn

Thomas H Hunn (active 1878-1910)

Thomas Hunn lived in Hackney and later in Surrey. He painted in the Home Counties, and exhibited the results at the Royal Academy and the Royal Society of British Artists.

56. Silver Birch River

signed, watercolour, 14 ½ x 10 inches

Cecil Arthur Hunt

Cecil Arthur Hunt, VPRWS RBA (1873-1965)

For a biography of Cecil Arthur Hunt, please refer to *Chris Beetles Summer Show*, 1998, page 93.

57. Caerphilly Castle, Wales

signed and inscribed 'Castle Wales', watercolour and bodycolour, 11 ¼ x 15 ¾ inches

Hunt visited Caerphilly Castle on a tour of Southern Wales in 1927 (Sketchbook 12). The view shows the leaning South East Tower and Gatehouse prior to the restoration by the Bute family in the 1950s.

58. Coulmore

signed and inscribed with title, watercolour and bodycolour, 11 x 15 inches; watercolour on reverse, signed and inscribed 'Glencoe'

59. The Jura

signed, watercolour, 8 ½ x 10 ¾ inches

60. Trees by the Water's Edge

signed, watercolour, 14 x 20 ½ inches

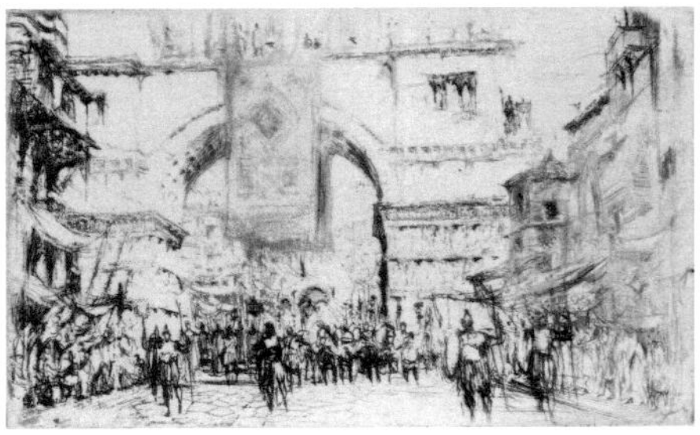
61

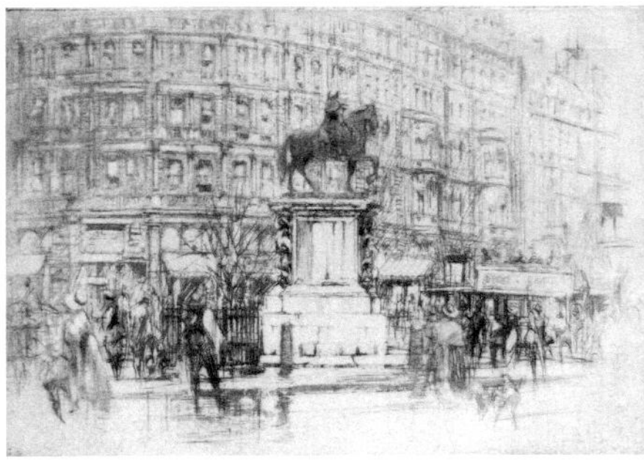
62

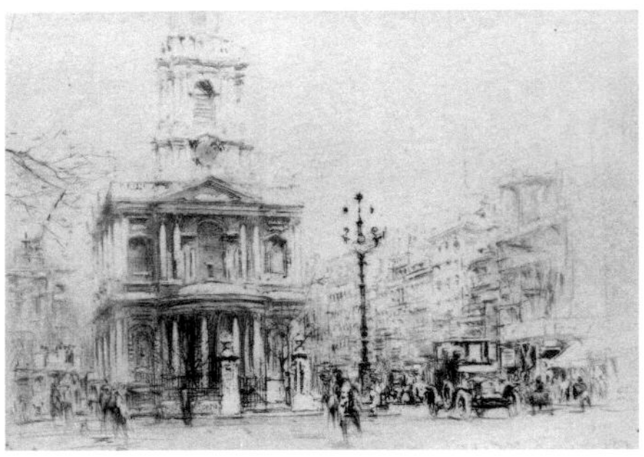
63

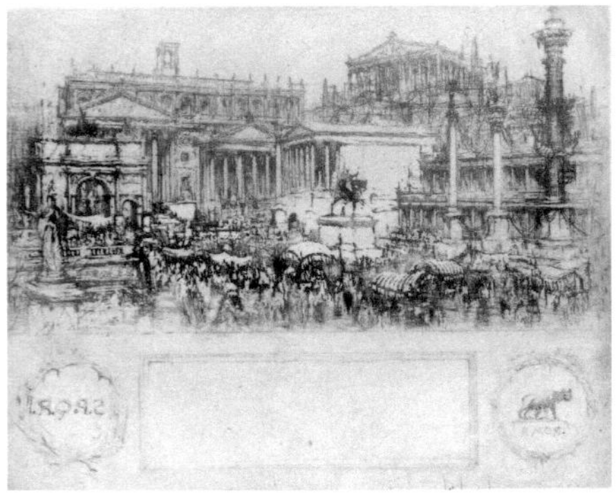
64

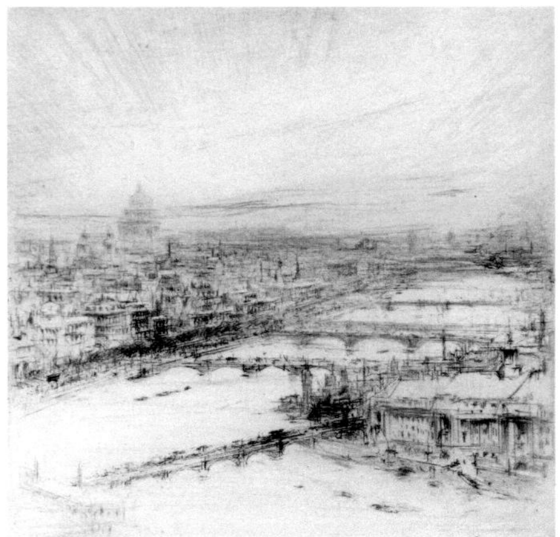
65

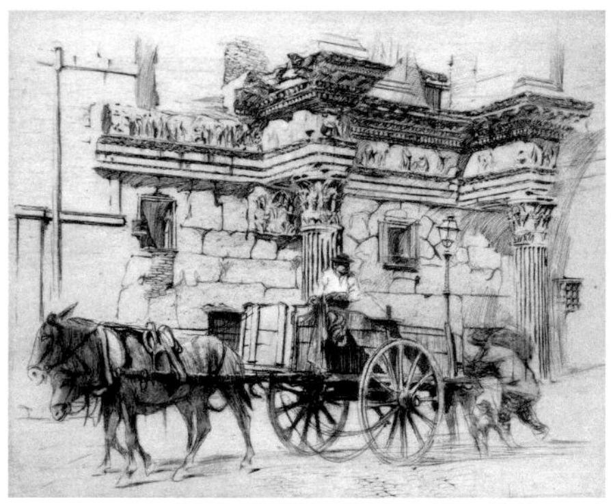
66

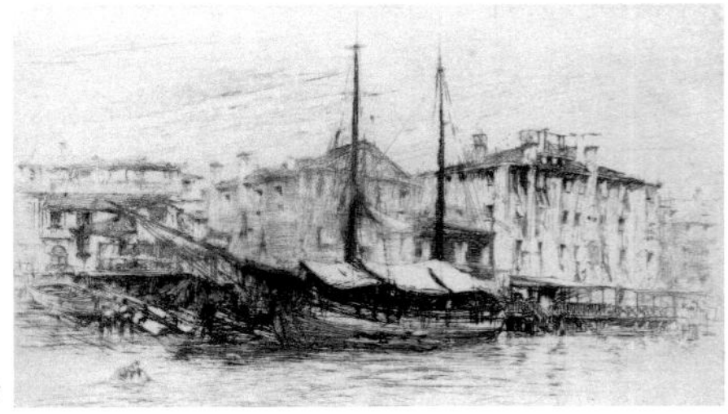
67

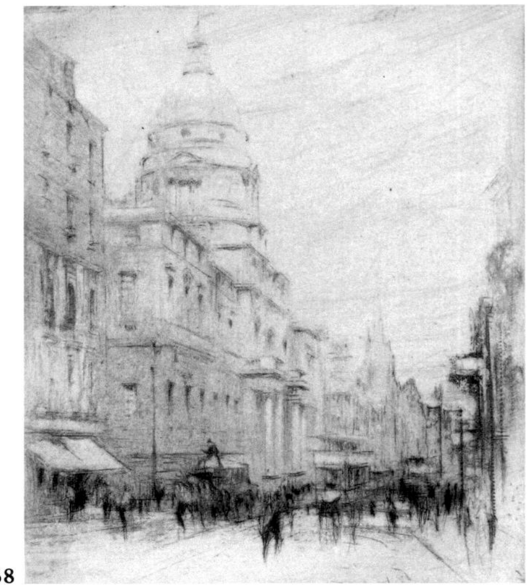
68

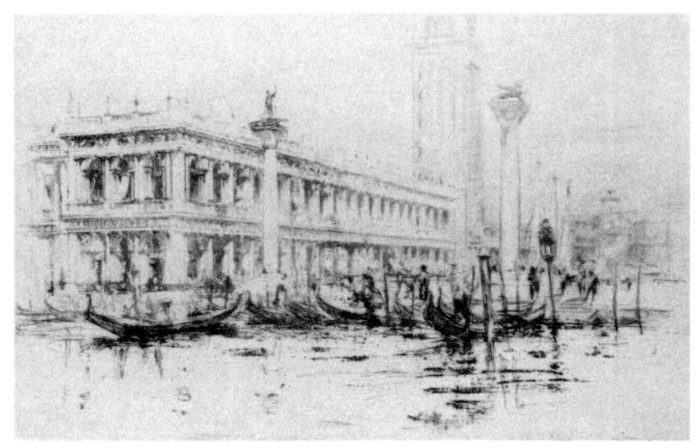
69

William Walcot

William Walcot, RBA RE (1874-1943)

For a biography of William Walcot, please refer to page 34

61. The Entry of the Emperor Hadrian into Ancient Salonika
signed, etching, 3 ¼ x 5 inches

62. King Charles's statue, Charing Cross
signed, etching, 3 ½ x 5 inches

63. St Clement Danes
signed, etching with drypoint, 5 x 7 inches

64. The Forum, Ancient Rome
signed, etching, 4 ¾ x 4 ¾ inches

65. Over the Thames
signed, etching with drypoint, 5 x 4 ¾ inches

66. The Forum of Minerva
signed, etching with drypoint, 9 ½ x 11 ¼ inches

67. Moorings, Venice
signed, etching with drypoint, 4 x 6 ¾ inches

68. Princes Street, Edinburgh
signed, etching, 4 ¼ x 3 ½ inches

69. The Library of St Marks
signed, etching and drypoint on wove, 4 ¾ x 7 inches

70
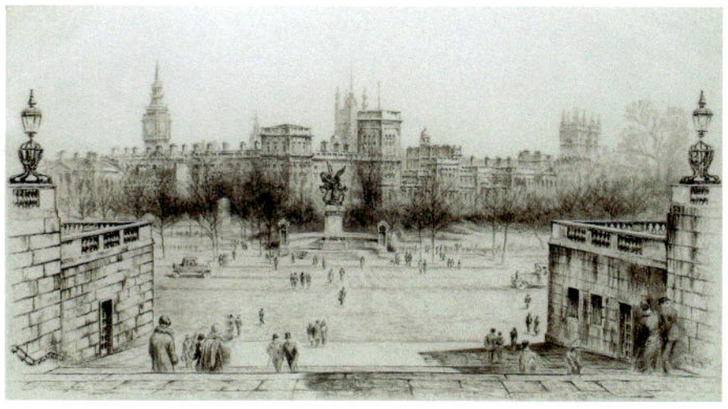

71
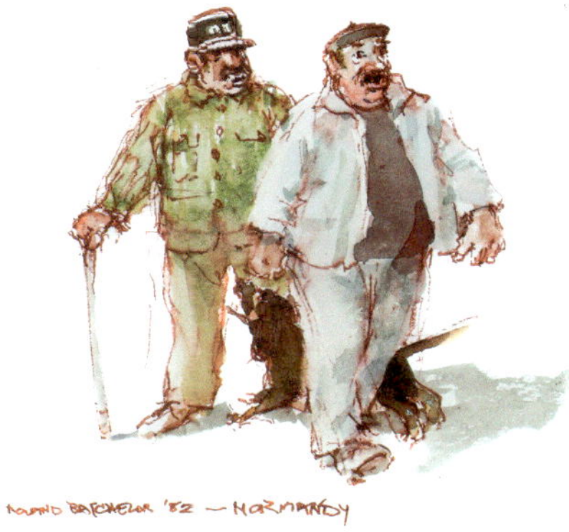

72
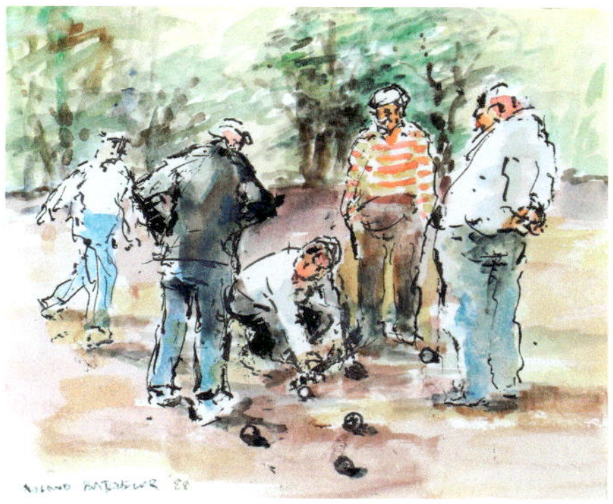

73
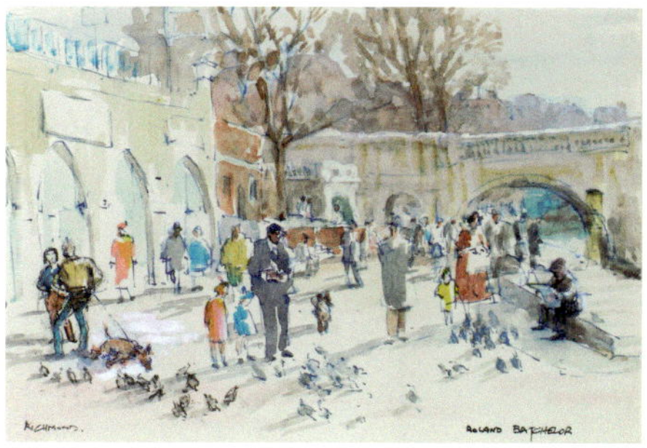

74
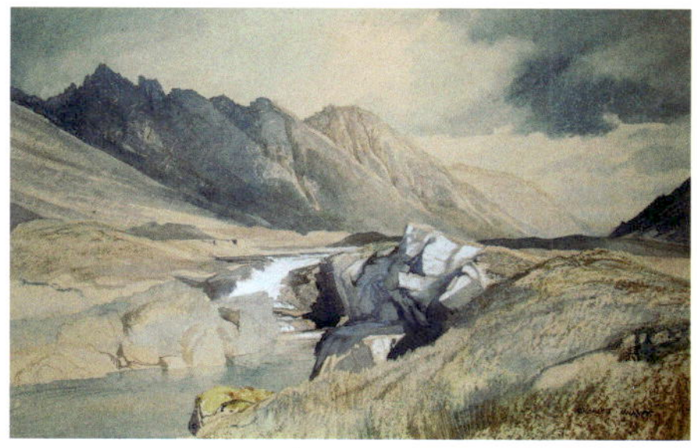

75
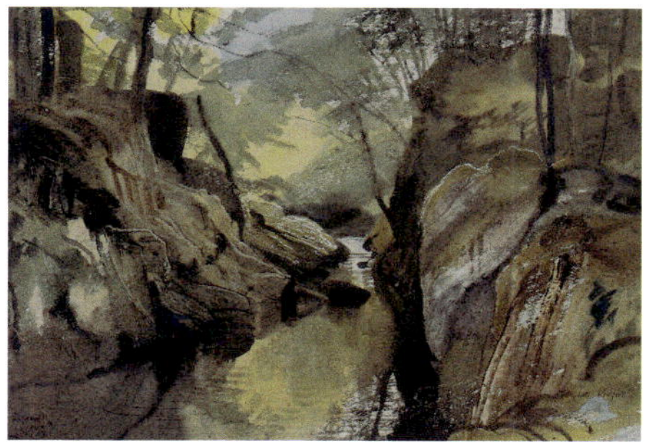

76
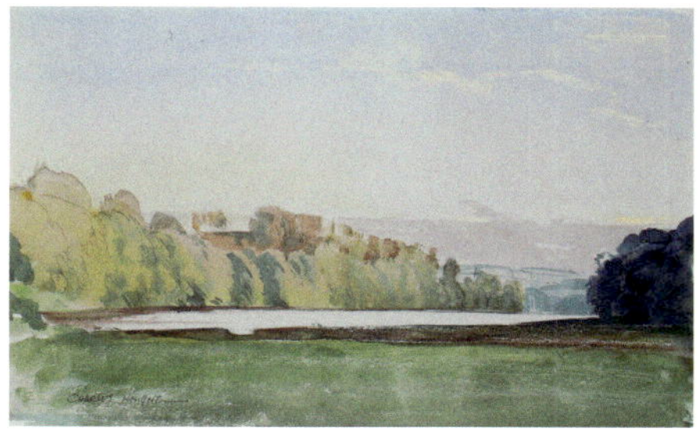

Fred Farrell

Frederick Arthur Farrell (1882-1935)

Largely self-taught as an artist, Fred Farrell specialised in paintings and etchings of British and European townscapes, in a style that seems to have been influenced by Muirhead Bone. His watercolours and illustrations of First World War subjects are equally evocative. He lived mainly in Glasgow and exhibited at the Glasgow Institute.

70. Duke of York's Steps, The Mall

signed, stamped with the blind stamp of The Fine Art Trade Guild, etching, 8 ½ x 14 ½ inches, published 1929, from an edition of 150 signed proofs

Roland Batchelor

Roland Batchelor, RWS (1889-1990)

For a biography of Roland Batchelor, please refer to *Chris Beetles Summer Show*, 1998, page 153.

71. Rural Normandy: A Brush with the Law

signed, inscribed with title and dated '82, pen ink and watercolour, 8 ¼ x 8 inches

Provenance: Patty Jarrett, the Artist's biographer

72. A Game of Boules

signed and dated '88, signed, inscribed with title and dated 'October 1988' on reverse, pen ink and watercolour, 8 ¾ x 10 ¼ inches

Provenance: Patty Jarrett, the Artist's biographer

73. Richmond

signed and inscribed with title, further inscribed with 'Sunny Day, Richmond' on original mount, pen ink and watercolour, 5 x 7 inches

Provenance: Patty Jarrett, the Artist's biographer

Charles Knight

Charles Knight, RWS ROI (1901-1990)

For a biography of Charles Knight, please refer to *Chris Beetles Summer Show*, 1998, page 134.

74. Chancellors Ridge, Glencoe

signed, watercolour with bodycolour, 16 ½ x 25 ½ inches

Exhibited: Royal Society of Painters in Water-Colours, Spring 1949, no 5; Oldham and Bolton, 1949; Brighton Art Gallery, 1951; *'More than a Touch of Poetry'. Landscapes by Charles Knight RWS ROI* (1901-1990), no 69: Towner Museum and Art Gallery, Eastbourne, April–May 1997, Chris Beetles Ltd, June 1997

75. The Long Pool on the Lyn

signed, watercolour, 15 x 21 inches

Exhibited: Royal Society of Painters in Water-Colours, Spring 1953, no 50; *'More than a Touch of Poetry'. Landscapes by Charles Knight RWS ROI* (1901-1990), June 1997, no 71: Towner Museum and Art Gallery, Eastbourne, April–May 1997, Chris Beetles Ltd, June 1997

76. River Dart

signed, watercolour, 8 ¾ x 14 ¼ inches

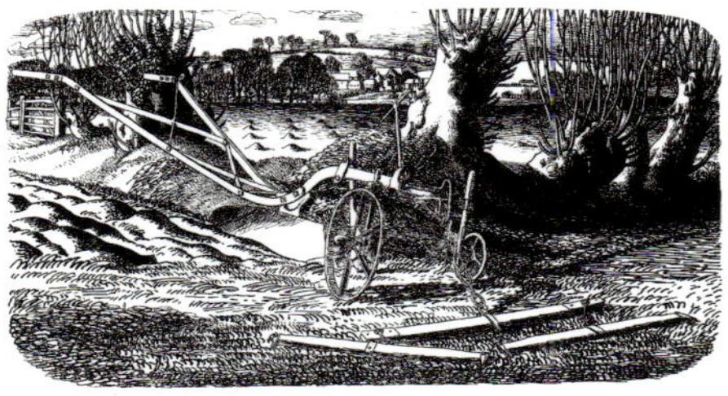

77

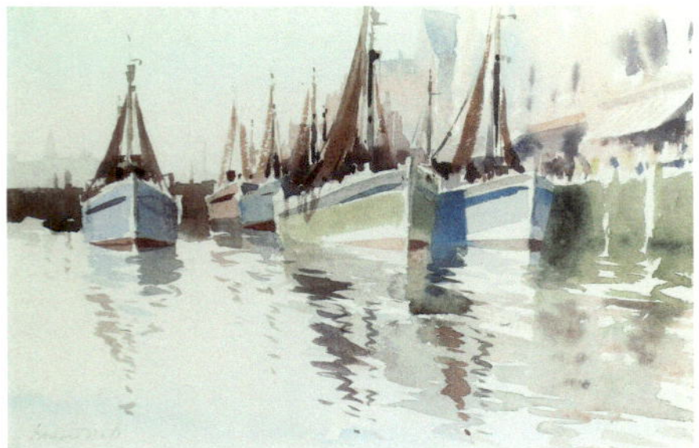

79

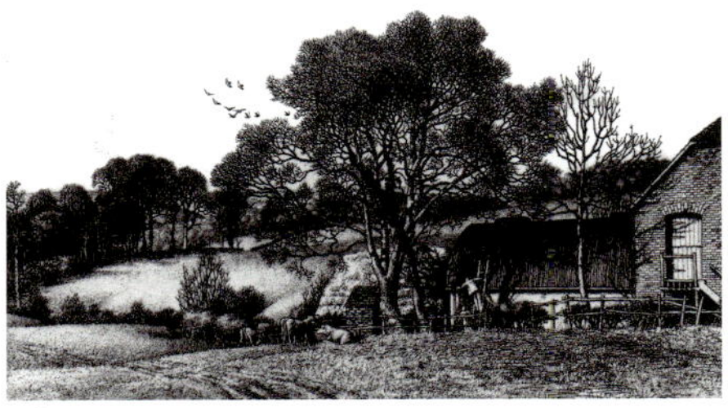

78

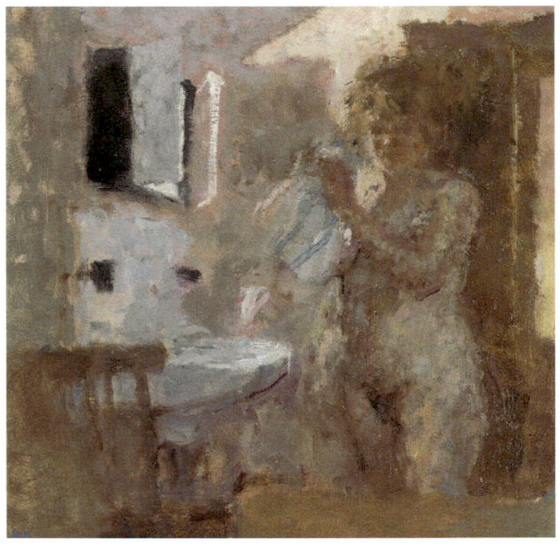

80

Stanley Roy Badmin
Stanley Roy Badmin, RWS (1906-1989)

For a biography of S R Badmin, please refer to *Chris Beetles Summer Show*, 1998, page 127.

77. The Plough
signed with initials, signed and inscribed with title and 'Near Bures. Essex' below mount, pen and ink, 4 ½ x 7 ¾ inches

78. Tanyard Farm
signed and inscribed with title below mount, etching, 5 x 6 ⅞ inches, number 10 from an edition of 40, executed in 1929
Literature: Chris Beetles, *S R Badmin and the English Landscape*, London: Collins, 1985, page 62, catalogue raisonné no 13

Edward Seago
Edward Seago, RBA RWS (1910-1974)

For a biography of Edward Seago, please refer to page 39

79. Fishing Boats, Ostend
signed, watercolour, 7 ½ x 11 inches

Bernard Dunstan
Bernard Dunstan, RA PRWA NEAC HPS (born 1920)

For a biography of Bernard Dunstan, please refer to Chris Beetles Summer Show, 2002, page 44.

80. Albergo Stella Night, II
signed with initials, signed, inscribed with title and dated '10.77' on reverse, oil on board, 11 x 11 ¼ inches

Cumulative Index of Summer Show Catalogues 1998-2004

I: Artists

II: Topography

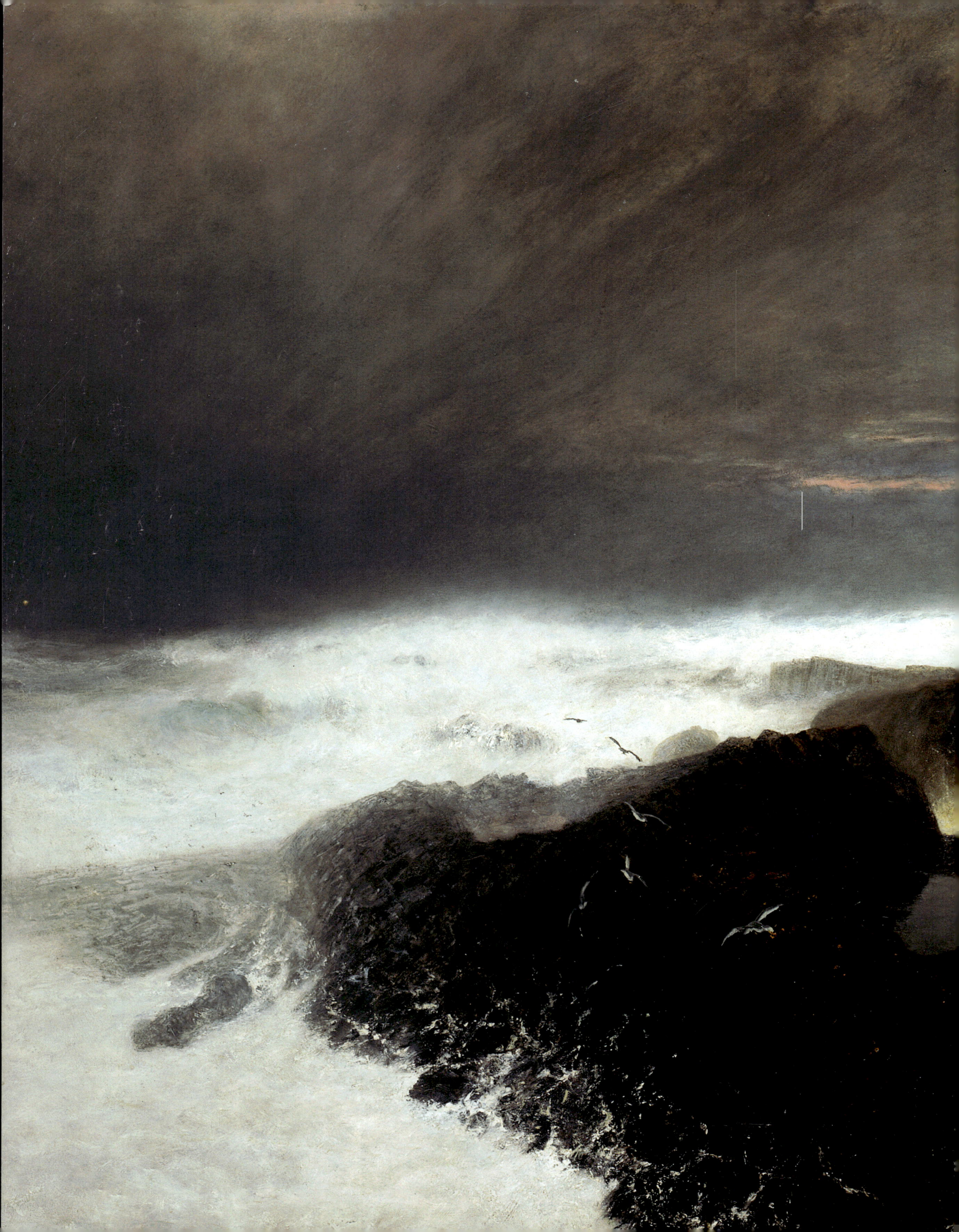